THE CYCLE OF

GRACE

THE CYCLE OF
GRACE

LIVING IN SACRED BALANCE

TREVOR HUDSON AND

JERRY P. HAAS

UPPER
ROOM BOOKS®
NASHVILLE

THE CYCLE OF GRACE
Living in Sacred Balance
© 2012 by Upper Room Books
All rights reserved.

Cover design: Bruce Gore/Gorestudio.com
Cover photo: iStock/Getty Images

ISBN 978-0-8358-1198-9 (print)—ISBN 978-0-8358-1229-0 (mobi)—
ISBN 978-0-8358-1202-3 (epub)

To Debbie, my partner in marriage,

Joni and Mark, our children,

for helping me find a sacred balance in my life.

—TREVOR

To Donna, my loving spouse and spiritual friend

(Song of Solomon 5:16),

and Sister Paula Thompson, OSB,

spiritual director and sign of God's unconditional love.

—JERRY

CONTENTS

PREFACE

In 1983 Upper Room Ministries developed an in-depth program for clergy and laity called The Academy for Spiritual Formation. Seeking an ecumenical Christian spirituality, the program includes silence, worship, lectures, small groups, and covenant commitments. The Academy made a huge impact on me when I attended in 1992 while I was pastoring a congregation in Arizona. When I became Director of this ministry in 1999, I felt called to extend this ministry to other pastors. Thanks to a grant from the Lilly Endowment, Companions in Ministry (CiM) was launched, which ultimately led to the development of this book and video.

The design team of CiM and I invited the Rev. Trevor Hudson from South Africa to come among us to offer his insights on pastoral ministry. Trevor brought the qualities we had been looking for: spiritual depth, commitment to social justice and inclusiveness, rich and delightful insights into what it means to serve as a pastor in a congregation today. Of all his excellent presentations, the one he offered on the Cycle of Grace resonated most clearly with the pastors in the program. On another occasion, clergy leaders in Arizona responded similarly to Trevor and to the Cycle of Grace. They formed a "little red writing group" to create materials for worship and Cycle of Grace groups, some of which is included here.

I extend appropriate thanks to many people who helped shape and encourage the development of this resource: Robin Pippin, Jeannie Crawford-Lee, Carmen Gaud, Pamela Hawkins, and Stephen Bryant, Upper Room colleagues; Sharon Ragland, Cynthia Langston Kirk and the rest of the Little Red Writing Group; John Wimmer and the Lilly Endowment; Harry Leake and other staff from United Methodist Communications; Sarah Wilke, publisher of The Upper Room who introduces the video segments; and most especially Trevor Hudson, whose friendship and many trips to the United States have enriched us all.

—Jerry P. Haas
Holy Week 2012

INTRODUCTION

For a number of years, as a Christ-follower and as a pastor, I lived the wrong way round. For reasons of which I am only partly aware, I struggled to believe that God really loved me. While I knew with my head all about the gospel of grace, the gap between my head and heart was vast. Deep down I felt that I needed to *earn* God's grace. If I achieved enough in my work, then perhaps I could get God to like me. It was a disastrous way to live. I started out trying to be fruitful, so that I could be significant, hoping then to gain sustenance so that I might be accepted. Not surprisingly, very early in my ministry I found myself living on the edges of emotional burnout and spiritual exhaustion.

Along the way, I received a treasure during my training in the early nineties with the UK-based Acorn Healing Trust in their Christian Listeners Training Program. There the Rev. Anne Long shared with us a simple model called the Cycle of Grace. Based on the Gospel explorations of a British psychiatrist by the name of Frank Lake and the well-known theologian Emil Brunner, this model described the balanced rhythms in which Jesus of Nazareth lived and ministered.* That gift-moment showed me that a more grace-filled way to live and minister existed.

Over the years, the Cycle of Grace has become a good friend. Not only have my own life and ministry been shaped by its insights, I have enjoyed sharing it with colleagues in ministry whenever possible. Usually its uncomplicated wisdom strikes a deep responsive chord. Those who hear about it want to explore it with others. Thankfully, someone who valued the richness of the model was prepared to invest huge amounts of time, energy, and competence in order to make it more widely available. That person was Jerry Haas of Upper Room Ministries. This resource expresses his faithful commitment to the soul-care of all involved in the ministry of the local congregation.

Jerry introduces the different dimensions of the Cycle of Grace so that you can either explore it on your own or with a small group. I have little doubt that you too will find it helpful. As I mentioned above, it has helped me to live the right way round. I would like to tell you how this happened for me. The Cycle of Grace, based on the life of Jesus, has four dimensions. It illustrates the continual resourcing of Jesus by the Spirit for Jesus' ministry with and to others. Here are several dimensions that I found most helpful.

The first dimension of the Cycle of Grace makes it obvious that the starting point for fruitful and effective ministry involves a clear sense of identity. This was Jesus' starting point. His public mission began only after he gained assurance in his baptism that his heavenly parent delighted in him unconditionally. Furthermore, throughout each stage of his life and ministry, he needed a freshly confirmed knowledge of his own identity as Beloved of God. This inward assurance of being beloved by God set Jesus free to be his own person, to pour himself out in extravagant self-giving, and finally to lay his life down in complete surrender on the cross.

I can still remember as I listened to Anne describe the Cycle of Grace how different my rhythms of life and ministry seemed to be. I was living and ministering in the opposite direction! I sought to gain a sense of acceptance from God through endless attempts to achieve more and more. Jesus' gospel invitation was clear: turn around and learn to live and minister the Jesus-way round. This is what I have been seeking to do ever since. While I still catch myself falling back into old ways again and again, the Cycle of Grace is always only a step away. I shudder to think how life and ministry would be for me without it.

The second dimension of the Cycle of Grace underlines the absolute necessity for ongoing sustenance in our life with God. I found it eye-opening to note the many ways in which Jesus was renewed regularly in body, mind, and spirit. Grace flowed into his life through many different means. Again the invitation was clear. If Jesus needed to be sustained in an ongoing way for life and ministry, then so did I. Like Jesus, I needed to find those ways that would best open my life and ministry to the nourishing grace of God and then build these practices into my life.

This dimension of sustenance in the Cycle of Grace also encouraged me to build my personal spiritual practices around those activities that nourish and bring joy to my life. It does not matter whether they are "religious" or not. Presently, my rule of life has practices like setting aside each Monday evening to be with my wife, going for a daily run, intentionally deepening friendships on a Friday night, and spending time alone with each of my children—besides my commitments to some solitude and silence, praying with the scriptures, and ongoing study. In all these ways I experience the grace of God sustaining me for life and ministry.

The third and fourth dimensions of the Cycle of Grace help us see that our personal ministry vocation requires answers to two questions: Who am I called to be? What I am called to do? The model shows that Jesus ministered through the significance of who he was *and* the fruitfulness of what he did. However, it also illustrates that *being* always precedes *doing*, an important sequence. Hence, even in his powerlessness on the cross, Jesus continued to minister through who he was to those around him.

This part of the Cycle of Grace has challenged me ever since my introduction to it. Not only have I sometimes limited my ministry vocation to those aspects I believe God wants me to do, I have also tended to put doing before being. This approach has often led toward placing my sense of significance in my achievements. Now I find myself trying to live the other way round. Over recent years it has been immensely life-giving and liberating to discern how God is calling me to be a sign of the love of Christ to those around me.

I do not want to say too much more. I hope though that I have whetted your appetite to explore further. Thanks to Jerry Haas you have in your hands an accessible resource that will help you to do this. It will introduce you to the Cycle of Grace and enable you to participate in its rhythms fully.

The implications of this model for our relationships, the way we raise our children, the structures of our congregations, as well as our personal lives are immense. I pray that the Spirit will use this model to help you, like it has helped me and continues to do so, to live the Jesus-way round.

—Trevor Hudson

*In his writings Dr. Frank Lake refers to this conceptual model as the Dynamic Cycle. It represented his attempt to correlate the dynamics of a well-functioning personality and spiritual health based upon the life of Jesus Christ. In my own presentations of the model I have relied on his pioneering work, while adding my own understanding of the life of Jesus in the Gospels.

HOW TO USE THIS BOOK

Rather than a single learning platform, *The Cycle of Grace: Living in Sacred Balance* comes to you with multiple entry points for your engagement. First, view the video with Trevor Hudson presenting the model, then read the corresponding chapter in the book. Next, journal your thoughts daily in response to the suggestions provided; finally, meet with at least one other person to share the journey.

The section in the book titled "Sharing the Journey" includes session outlines for six small-group gatherings. For two friends meeting informally to talk one-on-one, this may seem like more material than you can use. Be sure to read this part of the book, however; there's rich content you won't want to miss. And if you do organize or join a small group of three, four, or more people, the session outlines will keep you on track for six lively and fun gatherings.

In offering these multiple entry points, we hope that you become a participant in the Cycle of Grace, not just an observer of it. Your own vulnerability is key as you trust your heart to lead you in acknowledging and sharing the places that require your attentiveness to God's presence. While much of the book focuses on the individual's journey, the final chapter suggests ways the Cycle of Grace may bring new vitality to your congregation.

To view the video segments, go to

http://books.upperroom.org/blog/book/the-cycle-of-grace

To view the video segments on the Web, go to the website (www.YouTube.com) and type the session titles in the search box. The video segments are titled as follows:

Cycle of Grace 1. Acceptance

Cycle of Grace 2. Sustenance

Cycle of Grace 3. Significance

Cycle of Grace 4. Fruitfulness

Cycle of Grace 5. A Grace-Filled Way to Live

O N E

Burnout, Jesus, and Grace

*"Come to me, all you that are weary and are carrying
heavy burdens and I will give you rest."*

MATTHEW 11:28

Watch the first segment (Acceptance) of the video *The Cycle of Grace: Living in Sacred Balance* prior to reading this chapter. Use the space below to take notes on what you hear. For your convenience, Appendix A contains a summary of this and each video segment. Then read the material on "Burnout, Jesus, and Grace."

Burnout in the Bible and Today

The term *burnout* is a fairly recent addition to the English language, dating back to the 1970s; but the underlying reality is certainly not new. Search the scriptures and you will find many examples of stress, fatigue, exhaustion, and misconduct that indicate the dynamics of burnout. Moses, struggling to perform all the functions of leadership, wears himself out before his father-in-law suggests that he designate others to share the load (Exod. 18). David, exhausted after many battles, crosses the line and commits adultery with Bathsheba (2 Sam. 11). Jeremiah struggles mightily with his call, confessing his weariness and even cursing the day he was born (Jer. 20). In the New Testament, Martha expresses irritation with her sister, Mary. Perhaps it's just a momentary feeling; or does it signal a deeper discord (Luke 10:38-42)?

Today we hear about burnout all the time. Government workers, schoolteachers, doctors, and nurses—the problem fills the airwaves. Pastors and church leaders are not exempt from this epidemic. Significant literature has been developed over the last thirty years describing the phenomenon while analyzing its physical, psychological, organizational, and societal roots. Often missing from this discussion is reference to spiritual and theological factors. Pastors are encouraged to practice better self-care with weight loss, exercise, and healthier self-talk, rather than "soul care" and prayer.

Both authors of this book have been touched by burnout—either personally or through colleagues. We are concerned about the well-being of church leaders and regular members who are cynical, tired, and caught in a depressing downward cycle. We offer this resource not just as a remedy for this problem; but more broadly to bring some of the healing energy and light we find in Jesus Christ to the ministry, to the church, and to the lives of ordinary people seeking hope and health in today's world.

In the video, Trevor refers to the work of British psychiatrist Dr. Frank Lake. Lake developed the model of psychodynamic theory that Trevor and Jerry refer to as the Cycle of Grace.[1] As pastors, both of them find this model helpful in reflecting on their own lives and ministries; thus they pass it on to you, the reader. When Lake teamed up with theologian Emil Brunner, they observed mission workers in India burning out quickly. They saw that when under stress, the mission workers' pattern of living differed from the pattern they witnessed in Jesus' life. Therefore, we begin by taking a closer look at Jesus' life.

Attending to Jesus

What marks the beginning of Jesus' ministry? Frank Lake summarized the answer in the word *Acceptance*.[2] Nurtured in the womb of a loving mother; raised by parents who provided protection, guidance, and care, Jesus "grew and became strong, filled with wisdom" (Luke 2:40). As an adolescent, he had a confident spirit, evidenced by his lingering in the Temple to sit among the elders and engage them in conversation (Luke 2:41

and following). The story then jumps from the twelfth year of Jesus' life to the thirtieth (see Luke 3:23), the year of his baptism. Divine revelation transforms the nurture of his childhood; at the river Jordan, Abba God announces the blessing, "You are my Son, the Beloved; with you I am well pleased" (Mark 1:11).

Jesus knew acceptance on a human level. Now he knows acceptance as a holy name and divine calling. This blessing has a profound effect. After his baptism, Jesus' ministry takes on the full vibrancy of faith: encountering the demons in the wilderness and in the demon-possessed; healing the sick and the lame; offering hospitality to the disenfranchised; teaching on the hillsides, at table, and on the mountain. Measuring the impact, a simple before-and-after analysis reveals the significance of Jesus' baptism.

Just before entering Jerusalem where he will meet his death, Jesus hears the Divine Voice addressing him as Beloved a second time: at his Transfiguration (Mark 9:7).

An Invitation to Acceptance

Acceptance may seem an inadequate term to convey the fullness of the meaning of God's grace. Perhaps no word is! Acceptance has different levels of meaning, however.

If a person's work is *acceptable* that generally means it meets the minimal standards required by an employer. *Acceptable* falls far below exceptional; often *acceptable* implies simply getting by.

If a person gains *acceptance* into university, we assume that he or she has met certain standards for grades and test scores. Such acceptance is conditional; one is accepted or acceptable if, and only if, the person meets or exceeds these standards.

Sometimes particular roles limit *acceptance*. In a popular TV drama, the chauffeur is accepted so long as he acts in his limited function as a driver. When he courts the daughter of the noble family that owns the estate, however, he stirs the father's wrath and is summarily dismissed from his job and from his quarters.

In today's culture *acceptance* often reflects a laissez-faire attitude. Our casual acceptance of someone we do not know or want to know may sound like acceptance, but it's really indifference. The oft-repeated comment, "Whatever . . ." gives the message, "I really don't care."

The best corollary to divine *Acceptance* comes in that rare human relationship where a person is fully known, valued, and loved; a relationship with a mutual sense of safety and trust. Both authors of this book have experienced this level of relationship in their lives at various times through mentors, family members, and friends. Jerry remembers meeting his spiritual director for the first time and feeling an immediate sense of warmth and welcome. Over time he experienced the freedom to be himself, share confidences, grieve losses, and celebrate new joys. By offering a glimpse of divine acceptance, this relationship helped him claim and reclaim his identity as child of God. A further sign of

God's grace is that acceptance, when received, begs not to be hoarded but offered freely to others.

Returning to the story of Jesus' baptism, we see this dynamic of God's acceptance at work. Jesus did not interpret what he received at his baptism—affirmation as God's Beloved—as just for him but for all. His life became a continuous outpouring of the acceptance he had been given. His acceptance became manifest in Jesus' listening to those who felt forgotten, welcoming the outcast and the stranger, and healing people—even on the sabbath! Jesus reflected God's acceptance of him and mirrored that to others. The grace that Jesus received became grace for all. Or as it says in scripture, "From his fullness, we have all received, grace upon grace" (John 1:16).

All are invited to receive the acceptance that God gave to Jesus. You've received the invitation; what's holding you back?

Cycle of Grace

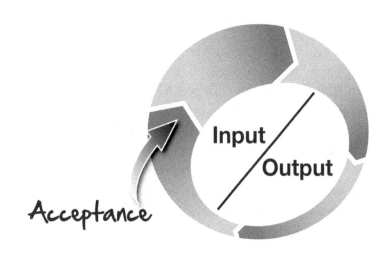

The Grace to Receive

Many hard-working people have a difficult time receiving gifts; they find it easier to be on the giving side. Jesus, however, demonstrated the grace to receive. When the woman came with oil for anointing, he accepted her blessing. When the child came with bread to share, he welcomed the gift and multiplied it. When he saw Zacchaeus in the tree, he didn't wait for an invitation but told him to "hurry and come down; for I must stay at your house today" (Luke 19:5).

Many people seem reluctant to accept God's grace. Marian Cowan addresses the hesitancy of church leaders and others when she writes, "It is so easy for us to tell other people that they are made in the image and likeness of God, but oftentimes it is difficult to accept it for ourselves."[3] She notes that those with a poor self-concept sometimes say to someone who has just complimented them, "If you only knew, . . . " To those persons, she suggests that "they hear God saying to them, 'If *you* only knew, you could not help but love yourself, because you are my very energy in human form. You are a burning bush, afire with my presence.'"[4]

In recent years, services of baptismal covenant renewal have become more common in some faith communities. No matter our age at baptism, these services serve as marvelous reminders of God's acceptance of us, a gift to be received. While many of us cannot literally remember our baptism, the words "Remember your baptism and be thankful!" stir us to draw on the blessing heard by Jesus and passed down to us. "From his fullness we have all received"; we too have been baptized; we too have received God's Acceptance; we too are the Beloved.

However reluctantly we finally receive God's gift of acceptance, God patiently welcomes us into loving embrace. The prodigal son didn't get a long to-do list when he came back to his father's house (Luke 15); Jesus, after his baptism, didn't get a list of strategies to wipe out evil. Acceptance ushers in a God-given identity, and God's Spirit guides the coming encounters. It's an exciting way to live!

Journaling Suggestions

One: Burnout, Jesus, and Grace

Day One

Who or what has helped you feel most completely accepted for who you are in your life? If a person, take a moment to reflect on his or her face, gestures, words, and silence that welcomed your whole being. Alternately, you may think of a book, a pet, a home, or a place in nature that communicated acceptance to you. Meditate in silence for a few moments, and then write down what you observed and felt.

Day Two

What's the difference between feeling tired and feeling burned out? Try to identify a time when you felt very tired, perhaps even exhausted—but not burned out. Some people call this experience a "good tired" feeling. What makes it feel good? Now reflect on a time when you felt burned out. How does your experience in those times differ? How might God be at work in your tiredness and in your burnout?

Day Three

Who has demonstrated to you "the grace to receive"? Perhaps you think of someone who knows how to accept a gift or a compliment. How can you begin to practice this grace in your life?

DAY FOUR

Archbishop Desmond Tutu, addressing antiapartheid protesters after a bloody clash with police in 1989, spoke these stirring words:

> Say to yourselves, in your heart: "God loves me." In your heart: God loves me, God loves me. . . . I am of infinite value to God. God created me for freedom. . . . My freedom is inalienable. My freedom is God-given! I don't go around and say, Baas [boss], please give me my freedom. God loves me, I am of infinite value because God loves me and God created me for freedom, and my freedom is inalienable, God-given. Right! Now straighten up your shoulders, come, straighten up your shoulders like people who are born for freedom! Lovely, lovely, lovely!"[5]

When have you needed to hear these words? How might you boldly claim your God-given belovedness?

DAY FIVE

Read these words from Isaiah 30:15. Let them soak into your soul.

> In returning and rest you shall be saved;
>> in quietness and in trust shall be your strength.

Reflect on the importance of rest in your life and how it opens you to receive God's acceptance. Spend the next twenty minutes in silence, resting in God's love. Journal what this experience was like for you.

Preparation for Sharing the Journey

The section titled "Sharing the Journey" (page 73) invites you to share with others some of what you have discovered in this first chapter and video segment. Before you meet, review the written material as well as your responses to the Journaling Suggestions. Know that whatever you share is always optional, never required. Review the "Guidelines for Sharing" (Appendix B, page 103); pray for the people you'll be with, trusting that Christ is present wherever two or three are gathered.

T W O

Sustaining Grace

With joy you will draw water from the wells of salvation.

Isaiah 12:3

Watch the second segment (Sustenance) of the video *The Cycle of Grace: Living in Sacred Balance* prior to reading this chapter. Use the space below to take a few notes on what you hear. Appendix A includes a summary of the video. Then read the material on "Sustaining Grace."

The Mystery of Sustaining Grace

On a human level, God has created us in such a way that our bodies need food, water, air, and protective covering in order to survive. While water and air may be pure gift without need of human interaction (at least in the days before pollution!), from the beginning of time food and clothing require human labor. The earliest stories in Genesis record this human activity: man and woman sewing fig leaves together; Abraham and Sarah preparing a meal for unexpected guests (Gen. 18). In sometimes elaborate and complicated ways, human beings interact with the stuff of nature to make clothing for protection and prepare food for bodily nourishment.

So, are food and clothing entities that we create or that God creates? The answer, of course, is yes! Both human activity and creation's bounty are necessary in the production of food and clothing. Consider food. It must be harvested, prepared, served, chewed, and digested—all human activities. At the same time, without the sun and the rain, the oceans and the rivers, and all the raw stuff of nature, the food sources disappear. We depend on God to feed us.

This analogy helps us understand God's grace in this second segment of the Cycle. While Acceptance signals the pure inflow of grace from God without human assistance, sustaining grace reflects a marvelous blending of human and divine interaction. God's grace is now within us, exhibited through our heartfelt desire to grow closer to God. Like someone who has fallen in love, we want to learn all we can about this Other and return again and again to share in the intimacy. John Wesley called such efforts "the means of grace"; more recently these actions have been referred to as "spiritual disciplines." The authors suggest the phrase *sustaining practices* with a goal of staying close to God.

Whatever phrase you use, remember that this too is grace, woven into our motivations and our will and emerging in all that we do to open ourselves more fully to God.

Cycle of Grace

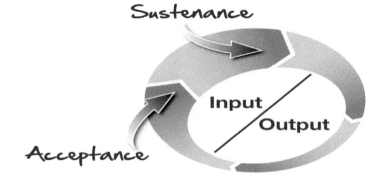

Sustaining Practices

In the video, Trevor raised this question, "What are some of the ways that Jesus sustained his close relationship with God throughout his life?" By phrasing the question this way, Trevor invites all of us to pay close attention to Jesus' life—not to slavishly imitate him but instead to strengthen our own relationship with a loving God. We watch and see how he sustained himself and so we learn how we might be sustained as well. We notice not only what he did but how he did it, and some of what we see surprises us.

The video-audience participants listed five of Jesus' sustaining practices. These and other practices are listed below:

1. He prayed.
2. He had a close group of followers, his disciples.
3. He worshiped in the synagogue.
4. He spent time in table fellowship with others.
5. He fed upon the scriptures.
6. He spent time in solitude.
7. He went for long walks.
8. He enjoyed God's creation, the world of nature.
9. He knew the value of rest and slept in unusual places (even in a sinking boat).
10. He welcomed children.
11. He related to persons considered unclean, such as lepers and the demon-possessed.
12. He spoke to women and to those not included in the Jewish faith.

More needs to be said about Jesus' relationship to others. A variety of people filled his life—tax collectors, Roman soldiers, the lame and the blind, desperate people and haughty people, adoring fans and scorning critics. From among them Jesus chose the twelve disciples. But notice that he sometimes narrowed the group to the three who accompanied him to the mountain or expanded it to the seventy who went out two by two. Jesus related to his followers in rich and varied ways. From his critics, such as the Pharisees, he seemed to draw strength, welcoming conflict rather than fleeing from it.

Trevor Hudson has often pointed out one set of relationships that we might easily overlook. John 11 mentions Jesus' love for Lazarus and for his sisters, Martha and Mary. Trevor suggests that with this family unit Jesus enjoyed a friendship of mutuality unlike any other in his range of relationships. Several exchanges in this chapter suggest an honesty of emotion we do not see elsewhere, as when Mary rebukes Jesus and when Jesus weeps. Is there even more to the story than what we read here?

Jean Vanier speculates that Lazarus would be considered disabled by today's standards and that Mary and Martha remained single to care for him. "The Greek word *asthenes* [the word *ill* in John 11:3] can be translated as 'sick,' 'without strength,' 'feeble' or 'insignificant.' . . . In the language of today, we would probably say '. . . disabled.'"[1] Trevor notes that Lazarus never speaks in this chapter or elsewhere in the Gospel; was he unable to speak or were his words simply not recorded? We don't know. No children or elderly family members appear in the story; three siblings comprise the household. Was this an unusual configuration for that time? Did it make a difference as to how Jesus related to them? We don't know. What we do know is that Jesus refers to none of them as a disciple, yet Jesus' love for them as individuals whom he calls by name suggests that each is an intimate friend. Trevor notes that these were three special friends with whom Jesus could rest and be cared for, which explains the familiarity among these people.

Reflecting on John 11 helps the reader see that Jesus valued friendships as one who received as well as one who gave. As a young person, Jerry remembers thinking that Jesus didn't really need friends. Yes, he served as a friend to others, many times; but did he receive from them? The hymn "What a Friend We Have in Jesus" tells about his availability to others, not about others' ministry to him. John 11 suggests a mutuality of give-and-take. In other stories we hear how Jesus drew upon the people around him to keep watch, to pray, to eat with him, and remain with him. Not all were faithful, but many of his friends and followers proved their faithfulness by gathering again when the worst had passed. When Jesus called his followers friends (John 15:15), he expressed not only a future hope but a current reality. Friendships and relationships of all kinds provided sustenance for his life. Through this rich social fabric and not in spite of it, he continued to connect to God's abiding love and grace.

Balance and Rhythm

As we talk about sustaining practices, we remember that in the first video segment Trevor mentions Lake and Brunner noting that Jesus' life had a certain balance or rhythm that they did not see in the lives of the mission workers. In the first video segment, Trevor read Mark 1 and noted the pattern of engagement and withdrawal in Jesus' life. We might keep in mind this overall flow of grace as we continue our discussion. Our relationship to God's grace is not static; instead it has an ebb and flow. More than a one-shot wonder, grace continues to work its way into and through our lives as we grow and mature in our faith.

Many Christ-followers have come to see the importance of sustaining practices as a way to balance the traditional emphasis on one-time conversion. Spiritual director Lisa Myers writes that spiritual practices help us understand that "grace is at work in the ordinary processes of daily activities as well as in the dramatic events of life."[2] Often the biggest challenge she says is to "creat[e] . . . theological space between justification and sanctification [to make] spiritual room for grace."[3] In other words, developing a spiritual practice involves theological as well as practical concerns, such as finding time in our daily schedules. In somewhat poetic language she goes on to say, "The practices, pro-cesses, and disciplines connect us to the deeper rhythms of grace and make it possible for us to begin to feel the dance and to embrace the identity and purpose that is ours individually and as a community."[4]

In other words, a conceptual understanding of Christian faith is not enough, just as a conceptual understanding of a good marriage or a healthy friendship is not enough. While many of us live a fast-paced life, faith, as well as love, requires a slower speed, whether it is learning the lessons of love on a human level or in relationship with a loving God. "Sustaining grace" means actively pursuing those activities necessary to keeping faith alive. And "sustaining grace" is also a fact: grace *does* sustain us if we let it; grace keeps us alive to the joys, riches, and challenges of life before God!

Journaling Suggestions

Two: Sustaining Grace

DAY ONE

One sustaining practice listed on page 29 refers to Jesus' enjoyment of God's creation, the world of nature. Consider such a practice for today's assignment. Take time to go for a walk, sit in the park, nurture houseplants, or simply "consider the lilies of the field" (Matt. 5:28). Journal what you saw, heard, smelled, touched, and felt.

Day Two

Review the list of sustaining practices in the chapter. In what other ways did Jesus sustain his intimate relationships with God besides those mentioned here? Page through one of the Gospels and make note of what you find. Use your imagination and have fun. One group listed forty-two ways Jesus seemed to sustain his relationship to God.

Day Three

Select one practice that you don't pursue or consider as a spiritual practice from the list you made on Day Two, and use it today. For example, if children are not regularly a part of your life, consider a way to watch or interact with them today. Journal about what you saw and how you felt.

Day Four

Read John 11, and pay special attention to the relationship among Jesus, Mary, Martha, and Lazarus. Notice how many times the word *love* is used to refer to Jesus' relationship to Lazarus or the sisters. What other words or actions suggest that the relationship between Jesus and these three siblings was especially close? Does your list of "sustaining practices" include the cultivation of close personal friendships? Why, or why not?

Day Five

John Wesley, founder of the Methodist movement, was known for his energy and activism. He traveled many miles on horseback and on foot to preach and guide the ministry. Sometimes theologians and historians lift him up as a kind of "energizer bunny" who never slowed down. Yet Wesley knew the value of rest and sometimes referred to sleep as a sacrament.[5] Take time today to rest, maybe even nap.

Preparation for Sharing the Journey

Review the chapter and what you have written in response to the Journaling Suggestions. Make note of any questions or comments you'll want to make. Since a meal is part of session two, note the change in schedule, dress, location, and so on. Ask participants to bring a Bible and a Bible concordance to the next session.

THREE

You Are a Sign

"Out of the believer's heart shall flow rivers of living water."

JOHN 7:38

Watch the third segment (Significance) of the video *The Cycle of Grace: Living in Sacred Balance* prior to reading this chapter. Use the space below to take notes on what you hear. Then read the material that follows.

An Inner Glow

Jerry tells this story:

> Some years ago I was coordinating a Five Day Academy for Spiritual Formation for lay and clergy leaders in my area. One faculty presenter had to drop out at the last minute due to a family emergency, so I was left scrambling to find a replacement. Thankfully, Sister Theresa agreed to come, flying in from across the country to give lectures on the Psalms. In those days before e-mail and Internet, I was not able to learn much about her except what a mutual friend had shared; no e-mail attachment with biographical information, no photo, no Facebook album, no Google search!
>
> Trusting somewhat blindly, I arranged for Sister Theresa's travel and agreed to pick her up at the airport. "How will I recognize you?" I asked over the phone the day before her flight. "You'll find me," she said confidently. Full of uncertainty I drove to the airport the next day. *Who is this woman, and why does she think I will be able to pick her out in the crowd?* I wondered as I pulled into the parking lot. Anxiously I rushed into the baggage claim area. People were everywhere, greeting family members, wrestling luggage, and looking for the exit. *Where is she?* I thought again impatiently. Then I saw her across the room. Away from bustle sat a woman with a warm smile looking straight at me. She had what I can only describe as an inner glow that simply shone in the midst of the chaos. Over the next five days of the retreat, I discovered that this inner glow came from a great love for God and a devoted practice of prayer. Sister Theresa was not hard to find at all!

How do human beings communicate? Scientists now know that we remember persons' body language more than we remember their words. Nonverbal communication, including posture, facial expressions, gestures, and tone of voice speak loudly to us. In this chapter of the book and video segment, the Cycle of Grace moves from "input" to "output" (see diagram on page 37). Grace flows into Jesus' life through acceptance and sustenance, and now grace flows around the circle under the word *Significance*. Jesus' significance suggests that he had an effect on people apart from his words. Why was it that they "left their nets"? Why did people feel that he taught with "authority, and not as their scribes" (Matt. 7:29)? Perhaps the answer lies in the presence Jesus communicated with every movement and breath.

While we have no photographs or videos clips of Jesus, he conveyed God's presence through his very being with an unmistakable inner glow. Think of his biblical forebear Moses, whose face shone so brightly he wore a veil (Exod. 34:29-35); think of his follower Stephen whose countenance was like an angel before his martyrdom (Acts 6:15). Jesus' own appearance was visibly transfigured through prayer (Luke 9:29). We can imagine that when he walked through a crowd, he conveyed the love, power, and grace of God with every step. Such was his significance—his very being was a sign of God's grace.

Cycle of Grace

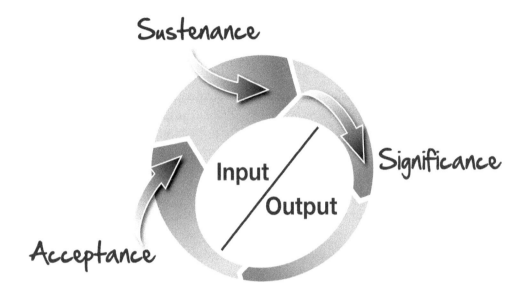

Sustenance

Significance

Input / Output

Acceptance

To Be a Sign

The root of the word *significance*[1] is the word *sign,* and so the question of significance is first of all the question, "What does one's life point to or signify?" Our materialistic culture emphasizes financial success, as if the most important sign of significance were the ability to buy whatever we wanted. Significance may also be measured by academic achievement, political influence, street savvy, business acumen, technological "smarts," or persuasive abilities. All of these point to competitive relationships, with the highest praise going to number one.

On the worldly level, Jesus' life seems insignificant. By the standards of the Roman Empire, his life didn't mean much. The Roman Empire existed before his birth and continued after his death. Yet Jesus radically alters the measure of significance. It becomes a truth one bears; a witness made; a life lived before God, desiring most of all to point to God. While many of us want to have a life of significance, as Trevor indicates in the video, fewer ask the deeper question, "What do I want my life to signify?"

In the video segment for chapter one, Trevor referred to Lake and Brunner and their stress on the importance of knowing who you are in order to engage in ministry. Here in this third movement in the Cycle of Grace, the issue of identity surfaces again. After his baptism, Jesus faced challenges in the wilderness from a voice that mocked him, "If you're really a man, prove yourself; perform; show the world who you are; be somebody; make a difference!" Christ overcame the Tempter's snare by remembering the inner Voice of love that had claimed him, "I love and accept you for who you really are, my Beloved." With an ever-deepening identity as God's Chosen, Jesus pointed beyond himself to the self-giving love of God. Jesus' own identity became Light, Bread, Life, Way, Truth, and Shepherd for a dark, lost, hungry, and superficial world.

The Gift of Your Uniqueness

What about us? All of us as Christ-followers are encouraged to "seek God's face" (Ps. 27:8) and reflect God's glory in our very being (2 Cor. 3:18). All of us can grow in our God-given identity. Through our brokenness, we humbly become "signs" that point to the greater "love which is at the heart of things," as Quaker writer Douglas Steere described God's presence.[2]

In their book *The Godbearing Life: The Art of Soul Tending for Youth Ministry,* Kenda Creasy Dean and Ron Foster describe the hunger young people have for "people whose own yes to God has transformed them into messengers of the gospel."[3] Writing to those who work with youth and to all of us, they say, "The moment we say yes to God, we become bearers of God's word. From the second we lower our defenses—"Here am I, the servant of the Lord; let it be with me according to your word"—the Holy Spirit enters us, fills us, takes us over, changes everything about us, and, through us, the world in which we live."[4] Such is our significance; we become God-bearers!

In his book *Discovering Your Personal Vocation: The Search for Meaning through the Spiritual Exercises,* Herbert Alphonso states that each of us has an "unrepeatable uniqueness" given to us when God calls us by name.[5] The writers of the Foreword to that book support Alphonso's belief that "the true purpose of the Exercises is to help us remember our real name, or 'personal vocation.'"[6] In other words, becoming a Christ-follower doesn't mean greater conformity; instead, it means greater eccentricity. The deeper the relationship with Christ, the more the Christ-follower's uniqueness begins to shine.

Biblical scholar Robert Mulholland grounds our unique God-given identity, our significance as Christ-followers, in scripture. While reading Ephesians in the original language (Greek), he noticed something unusual about the word usually translated *chose* in 1:4. The sentence begins with verse 3 and reads, "Blessed be the God and Father of our Lord Jesus Christ, who has blessed us in Christ with every spiritual blessing in the heavenly places, just as he chose us in Christ before the foundation of the world to be holy and blameless before him in love." The word *chose* here is composed of two Greek words, *ek* and *lektos,* which comes from the word *lego.* According to Mulholland, *ek* means "out of" or "forth from" and *lego* means "to speak." Therefore, the phrase "he chose us" can be translated "he [God] spoke us forth." Mulholland concludes that "every human being is a word that God speaks into existence."[7] We are unique and divinely created!

The inner glow of the contemplative spirit originates in God's unconditional love and overflows into the warmth of a presence so genuine that it defies mimicry. Over one hundred years ago people prayed for such an integrated way of being.

God be in my head, and in my understanding;
God be in my eyes, and in my looking;
God be in my mouth, and in my speaking;
God be in my heart, and in my thinking;
God be at my end, and at my departing. (*Sarum Primer*)

More recently, Mother Teresa prayed in this way:

Dear Jesus,
help us to spread your fragrance everywhere we go.
Flood our souls with your spirit and life.
Penetrate and possess our whole beings so utterly
    that our lives may only be a radiance of yours. . . .
Let us thus praise you in the way you love best
    by shining on those around us.
Let us preach you without preaching,
    not by words, but by our example
    by the catching force
    the sympathetic influence of what we do
    the evident fullness of the love our hearts bear to you.
                                                        Amen.[8]

Not all of us are called to minister with youth or in the streets of Calcutta. But we are all called to be signs of God's love, to lead grace-filled lives that have a significance the world does not know and cannot give. As we grow in understanding our own individuality, context, gifts, and call, we move from this more general way of being to the unique and eccentric goodness and style that we share. Far from stifling our individuality, Christ invites us to discover our particular way of being, our special significance, the gift of presence we offer the world.

Journaling Suggestions

Three: You Are a Sign

DAY ONE

Read the story titled "The Spirit Tree" on page 84. What signs of God's grace might you be overlooking (Gen. 28:16)? How might you grow in attentiveness and wonder to the world around you?

DAY TWO

In today's fast-paced, consumerist culture, people sometimes mask their feelings with a blank stare when riding on elevators or while waiting in line. When have you done this? Why? Compare this experience to those times when your face seemed to convey openness and receptivity to others. Journal your thoughts.

Day Three

In the video Trevor states that human beings have a need for significance. He goes on to say that each person has a unique way of being in the world, and he lists several examples. (See video summary, Appendix A, pages 98–102.) As you reflect on your significance, what do you think might be your unique way of being in the world? What song might your life "sing" to the world? What is its special message?

Day Four

Reread "The Spirit Tree." Notice that the author feels caught between two cultures: Western European and native Diné. Do you sometimes feel caught between two cultures, one that welcomes spiritual matters and the other that scorns them? What keeps you grounded in God's love and acceptance so that you can be a sign?

DAY FIVE

In the New Testament, those who were baptized were considered "marked" (Eph. 1:13; Rev. 7:3). Such a "sign" was considered a powerful protection against the forces of evil in this world. While all of us are vulnerable, at what times have you felt protected by Christ's presence in ways you cannot explain? Write a prayer of thanksgiving for God's care.

Preparation for Sharing the Journey

Review the chapter and what you have written in response to the Journaling Suggestions. Consider the special gift that you are to the world, the "song" your life seems to be singing. As you get to know the group, what prayer do you have for its members, for yourself, and for your time together this week? You are a unique and special person; give thanks to God!

F O U R

Fruitfulness and the Cycle of Works

Watch the fourth segment (Fruitfulness) of the video *The Cycle of Grace: Living in Sacred Balance* prior to reading this chapter which will be in two parts. The first part will discuss Fruitfulness, the final movement in the Cycle of Grace. The second part will discuss the Cycle of Works. Use the space below to take notes on what you hear. Then read the material below related to Fruitfulness.

Fruitfulness

But the wisdom from above is first pure, then peaceable,
gentle, willing to yield, full of mercy and good fruits, without
a trace of partiality or hypocrisy.

JAMES 3:17

We now come to the fourth and final movement of God's grace as it manifests itself in Fruitfulness.[1] We started by being rooted in God's Acceptance of us. We were then watered by God's Sustenance through practices and disciplines that strengthened our faith. We blossomed as Christ-followers by becoming signs of grace as unique persons, achieving a Significance we hardly thought possible. And now God's grace is transformed into an amazing Fruitfulness of our lives as we share God's grace with others. As we reflect on this fruitfulness, we begin as always by looking at Jesus' life and how this grace flowed through him.

JESUS' FRUITFULNESS

In the video we heard these affirmations of Jesus' Fruitfulness:

- Children felt valued and affirmed when they were with him.
- People were transformed by their encounter with him, using Zacchaeus as an example.
- Those on society's margins received God's love and acceptance through him.
- The disciples became—in spite of hesitations and errors—witnesses and workers who carried Christ's message to a needy world.

By the standards of the world, these achievements may not seem like much. Jesus did not leave behind a library of books, a new form of government, or a scientific formula. But his life had enormous impact! Page through one of the Gospels, and note other actions he took. You will find that they include the following:

- Teaching/Guidance—everywhere he went and with many different kinds of people
- Freedom/Love—offering a new way of relating to one another and to life
- Community—enriched by his presence
- Reconciliation—with God and between social groups
- Hope—for those who felt trapped in their lives and for those who were dying
- Healing/Release—touching the lives of many
- Purpose—calling people to participate in and to form God's reign and realm
- Wisdom/Discernment—a gift he often gave

- Rest/Blessing—to all who were weary or downtrodden
- Cleansing/Redirection/Forgiveness—new life
- Courage/Truth—including the courage to speak truth to power

This list refers to only some of the fruitfulness of Jesus' life and ministry. Perhaps the greatest fruit was the way in which Jesus modeled an intimate relationship with Abba, a relationship he encouraged us to emulate. We are all welcomed into the inner circle of God's love and acceptance!

Remarkably, Jesus' fruitfulness doesn't end with the New Testament record. You and I are beneficiaries; we become the fruit of his life and ministry through the gift of the Holy Spirit. God's grace and love extend all the way to the twenty-first century and beyond.

OUR FRUITFULNESS

As forgiven, reconciled, beloved people we can do many things that we never thought possible. We, as authors of this resource, have witnessed surprising periods of fruitfulness in our lives; as members of the body of Christ, we've also seen it in others. Times of immense productivity in ministry follow spiritual breakthrough and release. We sense the huge difference between those times when Fruitfulness comes from living out of the Cycle of Grace and those times when our own egos yield only "wild grapes" (to use the biblical image from Isaiah). Wild grapes are small, hard, and bitter; they provide no juice for the wine. Let us celebrate the grace-filled Fruitfulness of these and other people:

- Bill W., blessed by God's grace, founds Alcoholics Anonymous.
- Mother Teresa, discovering Jesus in the slums of Calcutta, establishes an Order to care for the forgotten.
- Millard Fuller, committed to offering dignity as well as housing, establishes Habitat for Humanity.
- Nelson Mandela, emerging from twenty-seven years in prison, extends reconciliation to political enemies and leads South Africa into democracy.

No example is perfect, but each shares the strong thread of grace woven in his or her life.

The Cycle of Works

He expected it to yield grapes,
but it yielded wild grapes.

ISAIAH 5:2

The Cycle of Grace reflects God's love moving outward, like ripples on a pond. When we stay centered on God's loving Acceptance, our lives bear Fruit that is beautiful to see and taste. But what happens when we don't? What happens when we begin by propping up our own image?

Isaiah prophesied in Judah at a time when the Israelites were not faithful in their response to God's way. Ignoring God they concentrated on their own wealth and achievement. Those with means exploited the poor, including the widow and the orphan. Proud of their wealth, these landowners added acreage to their vineyards and imagined greater prosperity to come. Yet the grapevines did not yield what they expected; the harvest brought only wild grapes, small and dry—not the fully fruited grape they wanted to make wine.

The analogy fits as we discuss the Cycle of Works. In the video Trevor reminds us of Lake and Brunner's concern about burned-out mission workers. Why were these missionaries so hard and bitter, like the wild grapes, when they had started out with such promise? Lake and Brunner diagnosed the problem in a way that brings insight to the conversation.

Cycle of Works

In this diagram we see what happens when people seek first to achieve, to be productive and fruitful. By starting there, they go counterclockwise, against the flow of grace, and become exhausted. Hoping to win "significance" (that is, prestige) they try hard to produce. If successful (so they say to themselves), maybe that success will sustain them and then others will accept them. Their ultimate goal is to gain acceptance, but acceptance that comes at a high price.

The video refers to *young* missionaries, but burnout can happen to people in any age group. No matter our age, we may fall into the way of thinking described here. The Cycle of Works has no age restrictions!

In chapter one we talked briefly about burnout. We may define this complex phenomenon as a long-term but reversible condition resulting in loss of energy as well as enthusiasm, accompanied by depression and cynicism. Physical, psychological, organizational, and relational matters also factor in.

By comparing the Cycle of Grace to the Cycle of Works, we also see that burnout is a spiritual matter. If we live as functional atheists, as though the only reality is the material world, burnout (or cynicism or despair) is inevitable. If we live in awareness of God's reality, trusting in God's loving acceptance, a totally different scenario presents itself. Not all burnout is the same. In Jesus' parable of the sower (Matt. 13), the sower scatters seeds on four kinds of soil. The seeds that fall on rocky soil sprout quickly, then wither and die. We may compare them to the young missionary workers who enthusiastically head off to India only to wither and die spiritually in a few months.

The seeds that fall among the thorns mature, but then other plants choke them out; and they die. We may compare them to another kind of burnout, the burnout that occurs after years in ministry, for example, when a slow, hard cynicism begins to form. Life's many distractions, past hopes, and unresolved grief crowd out the essential, life-giving spiritual nurture. One pastor describes this kind of burnout.

I never thought I'd be the victim of burnout. I managed my life well, worked hard, and enjoyed my congregation. I took care of myself physically, had a happy marriage, and continued to learn better ways to lead the church. Yet here I was in midlife with nothing left to give.

Gradually I came to realize that for me the core issues were spiritual. Seminary taught me how to think but not how to pray. While I had tried on my own to practice the spiritual disciplines, I had never been very successful. My relationship to God was much like Nicodemus in John 3. He was a Pharisee, well-educated, and probably overworked. Most of that sounded like me. Nicodemus sneaked away to visit Jesus at night. Like him, I also had a hard time owning up to my spiritual poverty. I looked for a long time to find something that might work for me. Finally I decided to attend a two-year Academy for Spiritual Formation, but I didn't tell any of my clergy friends what I was doing. I was exhausted, embarrassed, and hungry for God.

It was there that God came to me, fed me, and healed me through the lectures, the silence, the worship, and the prayers. During those weeks, I completely changed my orientation and simply fell head over heels in love—with God. As I continued in ministry after that experience, I learned to trust God's love and acceptance. I no longer felt that ministry was a battle between the congregation and me. It wasn't always easy, but I realized that when I started with God's love and acceptance, spent time in prayer, looked and listened for God's leading, ministry happened. At forty-five it seemed like my ministry was just beginning, twenty years after seminary. One other thing I noticed: the fear that used to subtly underlie my ministry was now gone.[2]

While this story comes from a pastor, laypeople sometimes experience the fatigue and restlessness associated with burnout as well. Learning what it means to live in the Cycle of Grace is important for all who feel the call to follow Jesus.

Journaling Suggestions

Four: Fruitfulness and the Cycle of Works

Day One

This chapter includes several examples of people whose lives bear witness to the fruitfulness of God's grace. Who else would you add? Try to think of people who have followed the flow of God's grace from Acceptance to Sustenance to Significance to Fruitfulness.

Day Two

Review the list of the fruits of Jesus' ministry. Which fruit do you believe the world needs right now? How can the fruits of Jesus' ministry be offered to the world more fully?

Day Three

In John 12:24 Jesus says, "Unless a grain of wheat falls into the earth and dies, it remains just a single grain; but if it dies, it bears much fruit."

What in you must die in order for you to be more fruitful? Are you clinging to some past failure (or success) that keeps you from moving on? What do you need to let go of in order to follow the way of self-giving love?

Day Four

Matthew 13 suggests two kinds of burnout: (1) the quick "flame-out" of youth (as with the missionaries to India) and (2) the more hardened cynical spirit of later years, exemplified by the pastor's story (see page 47). Some studies indicate that those in the age range of forty-five to fifty-five are most in danger of burning out. Why do you think this might be so? What do you notice in yourself as indicators of burnout?

DAY FIVE

Meditate on the following quotation from Simone Weil: "It is the light falling continually from heaven which alone gives a tree the energy to send powerful roots deep into the earth. The tree is really rooted in the sky."[3]

Bright and deeply spiritual, Simone Weil worked in a factory during the day but wrote profoundly insightful essays about grace in her free time. She studied science, and the process of photosynthesis (by which plants receive energy from the sun and transform it into growth) fascinated her.

What is she saying here about grace and what we need to survive in our daily lives? Take some time today to sit in the sun.

Preparation for Sharing the Journey

Reflect in your own life about the difference between living in the Cycle of Grace mode and living (or half-living) with a Cycle of Works orientation. What particular circumstances, people, words, or thoughts set off a Cycle of Works dynamic in you? What helps reorient you toward the Cycle of Grace? Look over your journal notes and the session outline for chapter four (pages 87–89) in preparation for your time with others.

FIVE

A Grace-Filled Way to Live

'Tis grace hath brought me safe thus far,
and grace will lead me home.

"AMAZING GRACE," VERSE 3

Watch the fifth segment (A Grace-Filled Way to Live) of the video *The Cycle of Grace: Living in Sacred Balance* prior to reading this chapter. It will serve as an introduction both to this chapter and to chapter six. Then read the material on "A Grace-Filled Way to Live."

Putting It All Together

Now that you have gained an understanding of the Cycle of Grace in its entirety, you may be wondering how to apply it—to your individual journey as a Christ-follower and to the congregation of which you are a part. We'll talk about individual application in this chapter and about the congregational application in the next chapter.

"Putting it all together" in the spiritual life begins by looking for a way to live that sustains you. The history of the Christian movement has referred to this approach as formulating a "rule of life." Beginning in the fourth century, desert fathers and mothers followed a strict ascetic lifestyle in hopes of developing the closest possible relationship with God. Silence, solitude, and unceasing prayer became standard practices for listening for a word from God. In the sixth century, Saint Benedict of Nursia took a balanced approach toward communal living with *ora et labora*, prayer and physical labor. The Rule of Saint Benedict is perhaps the best-known rule in the Western church and remains an invaluable source for Christian living today. Protestant reformers Martin Luther and John Calvin, revivalist John Wesley, and contemporary leaders such as Martin Luther King Jr., Pope John XXIII, and Desmond Tutu all created rules to guide their daily lives. Most rules include time for prayer, scripture reading, and silence. Journaling is a popular addition today; so too are practices related to physical health (exercise and diet). And while rules often have a contemplative tone, some include more extraverted practices such as conversation with a spiritual friend, blogging, and participation in small groups.

Marjorie J. Thompson, in her book *Soul Feast: An Invitation to the Christian Spiritual Life,* concludes her discussion of classic Christian disciplines with a chapter on developing a rule of life.[1] She begins by suggesting that the word *rule* can convey a harsh or restrictive image. We might prefer to consider the image of a trellis, such as the kind used in gardening to support plants and flowers. The trellis guides and supports growth. Similarly, we need a trellis to support our spiritual life, providing structure and balance to maximize our potential. The image of the trellis resonates with our need for encouragement to pursue a spiritual life in a culture dominated by materialistic and consumerist perspectives. It softens the notion of a "rule" with its connotation of punitive judgment. Yet the image of trellis does not convey everything that's needed. As every gardener knows, the plant needs not only support; it needs food, water, sunshine, and an occasional pruning.

Whatever image we use—rule, trellis, or another—creating an intentional pattern for the spiritual life carries immense benefits. The Cycle of Grace helps us create the sacred balance necessary in today's frantic and conflicted world. Formulating a rule begins not by trying hard to reach God but by observing God's work of Acceptance, Sustenance, Significance, and Fruitfulness. The Cycle of Grace reminds us that God was at work, moving through all of creation—before our birth and before earth's formation—offering life as pure gift, prior to all human willing or doing. God offers a gracious invitation to step into this life, to embrace it, and to live fully. The proof of that invitation is Jesus. His way of life serves as a model from which those who seek to follow him can learn and grow. From our birth through the years of growth, no matter our life course, no matter how much energy we expended for education or how much success we enjoyed in our vocation, God's grace is prior, working within us, all around us, and even through us—just as it did for Jesus. Thanks be to God!

Do you remember the play *Our Town* by Thornton Wilder? At the end of the first act, Rebecca tells George about a letter sent to

> "Jane Crofut; The Crofut Farm; Grover's Corners; Sutton County; New Hampshire; United States of America; . . . Continent of North America; Western Hemisphere; the Earth; the Solar System; the Universe; the Mind of God—that's what it said on the envelope." She ends breathlessly.
> "What do you know!" George exclaims.
> "And the postman brought it just the same." She says amazed.[2]

When we talk about formulating a rule of life, we begin by remembering where we live—not just in Grover's Corners but in the Mind of God.

Jesus knew this truth, a truth we often forget. Just before Jesus washed the disciples' feet, we read, "Jesus, *knowing . . . that he had come from God and was going to God*, got up . . . and tied a towel around himself. . . . Then he . . . began to wash the disciples' feet" (John 13:3-5, emphasis added). These few verses provide a succinct version of the Cycle of Grace: Jesus, grounded in God, bears witness to the love that is home for all of us.

Where to Begin: Declutter

If grace is the context of our lives, where do we begin to formulate a pattern for living a more grace-filled way of life? As this book is being written, Jerry and his spouse, Donna, are preparing to sell their home. Their realtor has encouraged them to "stage" the house for a quicker sale. Staging allows the prospective buyer to better see the house for its own sake, which means the seller needs to remove those little piles of stuff in the corner that so easily accumulate, as well as some of the furniture. The realtor's mantra for getting started is "declutter, declutter, declutter!"

By clearing away physical and mental distractions, we make space for grace; we create room for God to dwell within us. Decluttering opens the soul so that God may abide with us and we may abide with God.

Spiritual decluttering has several dimensions. In contemporary society we easily become distracted and lose our desire for God. Our obsession with material possessions may allow little "space for grace" to operate in our lives. A simplified lifestyle with more modest accruements opens up new possibilities for growing in our relationship with God.

Spiritual decluttering may relate to other attitudes and behaviors. Roger Owens in his book *Abba, Give Me a Word* confesses that his need for control kept him from trusting the living, moving Spirit of God who might take him where he did not want to go![3] Schedules, role expectations, and rigid planning can blind us to God's presence in the everyday.

As the first act in forming a pattern for living, the practice of decluttering expresses the confidence that we live in grace; that God is our home address, as Thornton Wilder put it. If we have encased ourselves in attitudes, behaviors, or stuff out of fear, greed, or unconscious habit, we will miss "that love which is at the heart of things." Such Love is not ours to create so much as it is ours to discover. Or as Margaret Funk puts it, "We need not assert 'love.' It just happens when we remove the weeds."[4]

Next Step: Stay Close to Jesus

If decluttering is the *first* step toward formulating a rule of life, what's the next step? In chapter two we discussed the pattern of sustaining grace we witness in the Gospels. We began to identify some of the many ways Jesus nurtured the intimacy of his life with God in everyday life. We imagined him eating with Pharisees, tax collectors, disciples, and friends. We pictured him walking along the seaside and listening to those in need. We thought not only about *what* he did but *how* he did it. We reminded ourselves that the point of such attentiveness to Jesus' life is not to imitate his every move but to ask ourselves on a personal level: "How can I live my life in a faithful way, following the life of grace I see in Jesus?"

In other words, stay close to Jesus. But how do we accomplish this task in an increasingly cluttered world? Both authors of this book appreciate various efforts to "get Jesus out of the box" in film, fiction, and testimony. As an example, Jean Vanier's book *Drawn into the Mystery of Jesus through the Gospel of John* helps us see him through the perspective of persons with disabilities. While new translations and commentaries may be useful, it is important to include time to record your own thoughts, perhaps by keeping a journal. Joining a spiritual formation group that practices scripture meditation or *lectio divina* offers a great opportunity to grow personally; the Upper Room resource *The Meeting [God] Bible* provides guidance in this practice.[5] The Jesus Prayer, passed down through the Russian Orthodox tradition, moves prayer from the head to the heart. By repeating the prayer "Lord Jesus Christ, Son of God, have mercy on me a sinner" many times, the person praying may hear a response from the living Christ. Taizé chants, set to beautiful music, also make use of repetition to invite a deeper, heartfelt response to the Word. Both familiar and new ways of relating to Jesus have value. Both authors love to return to favorite Gospel stories. At the same time both of us find it helpful to incorporate insights and practices from other historic, theological, and cultural perspectives— from desert fathers and mothers to Charles and John Wesley to African American to

Egyptian Coptic to Korean to Native American to Feminist. In a thousand ways, in many languages and cultures, Jesus welcomes those who look for him. He calls them by name, "You are my Beloved; with you I am well pleased."

Time and Timing

Time is often the battleground in our lives. Listen to your inner voice and you'll hear the complaint, "I don't have time." "I wish I had more time." "When will I ever have time?" Yet time is surprisingly pliable, in spite of our obsession with chronological time. Here is Jerry's experience with time and timing:

> If I am in conflict with someone, I may worry and wonder how to defend myself the next time I see him or her. I create a scenario in my mind about what might happen and what I'd like to say. I rehearse. Then I see the person, and it's not the way I imagined it. I blow up and say more than I should, or I withdraw. The conflict continues and a new imagined outcome pops up in my imagination. Energy, focus, and a significant amount of time are expended fruitlessly.
>
> I first learned how flexible time is when I began a regular spiritual practice. After forty-five minutes, half of which was spent in silence, I'd get ready for work and find myself surprisingly eager. When people came to me with problems or complaints, I was more ready to deal with the issues up front—I was more assertive but also more compassionate. My forty-five minutes of spiritual practice helped me to engage and deal with issues immediately rather procrastinating, avoiding conflict and wasting a lot of time in the process. I discovered I had more time available than I thought and began to look for more of life's surprises and little joys.
>
> Over the years I've also learned that the time I need for prayer and meditation varies according to what's going on in my life. Sometimes I have found it helpful to think of monthly or even quarterly patterns for renewal, especially when the daily or weekly routine doesn't seem like enough.

Times of stress may require more time with God, not less. What if there's too much going on even to sit quietly? Glenn Hinson, a professor who held moderate views in an extremely conservative seminary, found himself at the center of a volatile conflict. Exposed to regular attacks opposing his stance and theology, he began taking long and vigorous walks every day. Those walks became his time with God. He transformed his inner fear and anger into a practice that benefited his physical and spiritual health! He stood his ground but did so without apology or hate.

Archbishop Desmond Tutu stood at the center of the movement to overthrow apartheid in South Africa. In spite of his social activism he kept a rigorous schedule of prayer. Every day at four a.m. he began personal prayers on his knees or crouched alongside his bed. At five he took a thirty-minute walk, followed by a shower. At six he was in his study for devotional reading and work at his desk. At seven-thirty he went to the chapel to recite Morning Prayer. At eight he and the staff shared the Eucharist. After breakfast and a morning of labor, he was back in the chapel for thirty minutes of prayer at one p.m., returning again late in the afternoon for evening prayer and at night for compline.[6]

The patterning of a grace-filled way of life changes with need and circumstance. Most rules evolve. Begin in whatever manner you can, following whatever prayer pattern you choose. Keep listening for the Spirit's guidance. If you've lapsed from the pattern you hoped to establish, start again. It is usually best not to attempt too much, and it's okay to try different approaches. Sharing your journey with others may free you from unnecessary guilt about spiritual disciplines and provide the prayer support you need for a more vital spiritual life.

Journaling Suggestions

_____

Five: A Grace-Filled Way to Live

DAY ONE

Pope John XXIII, convenor of the Second Vatican Council, was one of the most influential Roman Catholic leaders of the twentieth century. As a seminary student he listed twelve practices for his "rule of life," including the following:

- Devote at least a quarter of an hour to mental prayer [i.e., silent meditation] as soon as you get out of bed in the morning. . . .

- Devote a quarter of an hour to spiritual reading. . . .

- Before going to bed, make a general examination of conscience, followed by an act of contrition, and prepare the points for the next day's meditation. . . .

- So as to be constant in your observation of these points, arrange the hours of your day, and set apart the special time for prayer, study and other devotions, for recreation and sleep, after consulting with your Spiritual Father. . . .

- Make a habit of frequently raising your mind to God, with brief but fervent invocations.[7]

As you read this list, notice the importance of marking time throughout the day. What options from this list appeal to you, and which don't? How could you incorporate some of the wisdom for your own "rule"?

Day Two

Archbishop Desmond Tutu maintained a rigorous prayer practice throughout his days as a leader in the antiapartheid movement (see pages 57–58). During times of great stress, how has your prayer life changed? How has your prayer life helped you when the storms of life are raging?

Day Three

How might you declutter your life today?

Day Four

This week you've learned about the rule of life. You've seen examples of the rules that others have sought to live by. Today you're invited to write your own rule or way to live based on the Cycle of Grace. Write your response to each of the following questions.

What could you do each day to remember acceptance, God's unconditional love that calls you Beloved?

What practice might you now include for greater sustenance in your life (review list from chapter two, page 29)?

How might you seek to be a sign of God's grace in the world, witnessing through your personal uniqueness?

How might you let God's fruitfulness flourish in your life even more than it already has?

DAY FIVE

Look over what you wrote yesterday and rest in the knowledge that you live in the context of grace; remember that your address is "the Earth; the Solar System; the Universe; the Mind of God."

Preparation for Sharing the Journey

Review the chapter and what you have written in response to the Journaling Suggestions. Make a note of any questions or comments you'll want to make. Take another look at your responses on Day Four as you seek to form or deepen your own pattern for a grace-filled way to live.

SIX

Congregational Vitality and the Cycle of Grace

"Is there then no more promise for Your Church?
Will its only ministry be to bury people?"

MICHEL BOUTTIER, PRAYERS FOR MY VILLAGE*

A portion of the fifth segment of the video *The Cycle of Grace: Living in Sacred Balance* refers to this discussion. If you have not watched it, do so now and then read the material on "Congregational Vitality and the Cycle of Grace."

Congregational Vitality

Michel Bouttier was a Protestant pastor in France during the 1950s. His lament (above), inspired by Psalm 130, conveys the prayerful hope of all who know the promise the gathered people of God can offer to one another and to the world. The gathered community of faith, the body of Christ on earth, plays a special role in incarnating truth. Yet much deters the church from this possibility: unhealthy and unresolved conflict within denominations, increasing isolation as individuals and families, and apathy and hostility toward religion in contemporary society—to name a few factors.

Over the last thirty years, congregational vitality has been a topic of much interest. After initial discussions related to church growth, many leaders focused on systems theory and "healthy" congregations. Dorothy Bass, Craig Dykstra, and others have identified the importance of spiritual practice, and Diana Butler Bass has researched "practicing" congregations. These conversations have been helpful, in our opinion. Less helpful are denominational efforts to assess congregational vitality based solely on numbers. Such a focus may add to the potential for burnout among pastors and lay leaders already burdened by decades of decline. Are numbers the best way to assess a congregation's vitality? How might reflection on the Cycle of Grace contribute to this conversation?

A Place for Grace?

As experienced local church pastors, both authors of this book have led retreats for congregational leaders. Introducing the Cycle of Grace at these retreats has often been one of the more popular sessions, focusing as it does on the vitality of individual church leaders, clergy or lay. As mentioned in the video, however, the Cycle of Grace can also be used to reflect on the vitality of congregations. Asking people where they experience acceptance in their church, for example, can lead to valuable conversation. The overall issue is this: Is your congregation a place for grace, or is it caught up in a "cycle of works" mentality?

Here are some possible questions (Q) for assessing your congregation around the four movements in the Cycle of Grace. Also included here are suggestions (S) for encouraging a greater responsiveness to the living God in your congregation:

ACCEPTANCE

Q: Where and how do people in your congregation gain a sense of God's unconditional Acceptance?

- o How would newcomers to your congregation answer this question? Were they welcomed when they first came? Was the spirit of hospitality extended to them in an ongoing loving way or did they (for example) feel pressured to join?

- How would those who have been in your congregation longer respond? Have they memories of congregational gatherings (worship, events, etc.) where God's acceptance seemed particularly real? What are their relationships like with other members of the congregation? Honest and loving or superficial and trite?
- What about those who have taken on major roles of leadership in the church? Do they balance the many hours on committees with time for sabbath rest? Have they become somewhat cynical under the burden of their responsibilities, or do they continue to find places for receiving the nurture they need as beloved children of God?

S: What might be done intentionally to offer a place for God's acceptance in your congregation? Possibilities include the following:

- Retreats especially for leaders but also for those new to the congregation.
- Celebratory worship services, particularly around Christmas and Easter, affirming God's love and forgiveness.
- Worship reaffirming the baptismal covenant as a sign of God's acceptance.

SUSTENANCE

Q: Where and how are members of the congregation encouraged to nurture their life with God through sustaining practices?

- How would those new to the congregation respond to this question? If they are new to the Christian faith, perhaps your church is where they heard the Lord's Prayer for the first time.
- How would those who have been in attendance longer respond? What opportunities have they had to learn a new spiritual practice, such as meditating on scripture (*lectio divina*)?
- How have congregational leaders continued to nurture their life with God even as they've assumed organizational responsibilities? Church meetings that include time for nurturing a sense of spiritual community through faith sharing, silence, and prayer are often judged by participants as much more valuable (and even efficient) than the usual business model.

S: What might be done to encourage Sustaining Grace?

- o Lent is a good time in the church's calendar to emphasize sustaining practices, providing the focus remains on grace and not on the "shoulds" and "oughts" that can so easily kill the spirit.
- o Small groups for spiritual formation are often the key to help individuals discover the practices that work for them. Three types of small groups may be considered: (a) open groups for spiritual conversation using a resource such as *The Upper Room* daily devotional guide or *Alive Now*; (b) short-term groups with an expectation of participation for six, eight, or twelve weeks (such as this resource); or (c) longer-term groups with a high level of commitment and confidentiality such as the Companions in Christ® series developed by The Upper Room. Most Upper Room Ministries publications can be used with a small group.
- o The Academy for Spiritual Formation® is an Upper Room program developed in 1983 for highly committed lay and clergy leaders with a strong desire to grow in their relationship with God.

SIGNIFICANCE

Q: Where and how do people in the congregation have a sense of God's Significance shining through your congregation?

- o Newcomers may tell you what they saw and felt when they first came to the church or even what they heard about the church before they arrived.
- o Those who have been in the congregation longer may identify a sense of the congregation's uniqueness. What witness does the congregation make, and who communicates the congregation's identity?
- o Those with long-term membership and leadership experience may have stories to tell about the congregation. How does this history witness to God's grace?

S: What might be done to encourage a greater sense of Significance?

- o A congregation's history can be told from the perspective of grace rather than building projects and pastoral tenure. Think of the Book of Acts, not First and Second Chronicles! A story such as "Bonded" by Gary Kennedy (page 93) communicates more of what God is

doing in a congregation than the statistical charts in the denominational report!

o Consider what this story says about a congregation's significance:
Shortly after 9/11, threats and violence against Muslims escalated in
the US. Muslims, especially women, were frightened and hesitated
to go out for fear of harassment. After learning about this situation,
women from a United Methodist congregation in Tucson decided
to accompany Muslim women to the market to provide a measure
of protection from this threat. Is this not what it means to be a sign
of God's love for the world?

FRUITFULNESS

Q: What might be signs of God's Fruitfulness in a congregation?

o Robert C. Morris suggests an assessment based on Galatians 5:22–
23, the Fruit of the Spirit (Appendix C, pages 105–107). Such an
assessment could be offered to the three groups already mentioned:
newcomers, regular members, and congregational leaders. How
would each group differ in its responses?

S: How might Fruitfulness be encouraged in a congregation?

o Intentional listening to members as part of the volunteer recruit-
ment process pays untold benefits. Such listening may be done in
small discernment groups or by trained volunteers. Listen not just
to the words but to the longings of the heart. The businessman may
not be the best choice for the finance committee if this is already his
burden from work. He may instead welcome a chance to work with
young people or in the nursery.

o Periodic reassessment of the congregation's vitality may help leaders
decide if they are caught in a Cycle of Works mentality. Do leaders
feel a push/pull with the congregation, a sense of nagging or cynicism? Are they caught in a subconscious effort to compete in the
numbers game with other congregations in the denomination? Pri-
oritizing fruitfulness may undercut the whole movement of grace in
a congregation's life.

o The language of corporations and business may deplete the congregation's sense of vitality. For example, some have used the term *cus-
tomers* to describe those who attend the church. This term reduces
the covenantal aspect of the relationship and sets up an artificial

relationship between the staff (who become the vendors) and the average churchgoer.

Assessing Grace

As you learn how to apply the Cycle of Grace to a local congregation, you may wonder whether this provides a valid assessment. After all, aren't these qualities highly subjective and therefore true only in the eyes of the beholder?

While it is true that God's grace *cannot* be measured, the congregation's sense of God's grace in its fourfold dimension can be. Assessments move beyond pure subjectivity when shared by a sizable group of people. This is the essence of social science: measuring human understanding and response. At their core, however, such measurements require critical thinking and much conversation. Statistics can assist the assessment process, but such technology can never be a substitute for the responsibility of the people of God to discern God's direction for their common life and ministry.[1]

Thoughtful engagement around the key questions raised by the Cycle of Grace can highlight how the congregation, with all of its diversity, perceives itself in the Cycle. Such assessments may strengthen rather than deplete congregational leaders who are often doing the best they can with limited resources to lead the church. Congregations can broaden the pool of respondents by using a piece of software such as "survey monkey." However, leaders should never allow technology to replace substantial conversation that often needs to take place.

Final Thoughts

The authors began this book with a concern about burnout among church leaders. We return to that concern as we write this final paragraph. We know how hard you work, how much you give to the building up of the body of Christ, and how faithfully you make a vital witness to the world. We pray that this resource has helped you; first in your own life, so that you may redirect and recenter yourself on God's grace; second, for your congregation that it might delight in God's abundant love and grace. May the God of grace, source of all life and wonder, fill you with peace! Go well!

Journaling Suggestions

Six: Congregational Vitality and the Cycle of Grace

DAY ONE

Where and how do you experience a sense of God's unconditional acceptance in your congregation? Assess your congregation by referring to the Cycle of Grace and the questions beginning on page 64.

DAY TWO

Continue to assess your congregation by referring to the questions on pages 64–68.

Day Three

Read again the speech by Desmond Tutu quoted on page 24 (chapter 1, Day 4 Journaling Suggestion). Imagine Archbishop Tutu visiting your congregation and offering the same speech to your people. How might his words challenge and inspire your congregation to be and do more than they thought possible?

Day Four

In Appendix C you will find a Congregational Assessment based on Galatians 5:22-23 (the fruit of the Spirit). Fill it out now, and be ready to share your responses with your group on whatever level you wish.

DAY FIVE

Michel Bouttier, the French Protestant pastor quoted at the beginning of this chapter, offered the following prayer for his congregation:

> Grant us, Lord, to be like an airfield for this village,
> constantly ready to receive You: the land cleared,
> the runway constantly retraced and leveled,
> where You might, at any moment, come to us and visit us
> from on high, assuring us of Your presence,
> Your love, Your sovereignty.
> Amen.[2]

How might your congregation become more like an airfield, more attentive to God's grace?

Preparation for Sharing the Journey

Review the chapter and what you have written in response to the Journaling Suggestions. Note any questions or comments you'll want to make. Be sure to complete the Congregational Assessment of the Fruit of the Spirit (Appendix C) and bring it to the session.

Sharing the Journey

"The virtuous soul that is alone . . . is like a lone burning coal;
it will grow colder rather than hotter."

SAINT JOHN OF THE CROSS*

Why Gather?

Because of the intensely personal nature of the spiritual life, you may feel reluctant to join with others to share experiences and perspectives. Who hasn't experienced small groups that diminish rather than enhance? Indeed, you may choose to use this resource—video, thought-provoking material, and Journaling Suggestions—as a private experience. Yet the spiritual life calls us into community, and we generally find ourselves to be healthier when we balance solitude with companionship. As Paul Tournier said, "There are two things you cannot do alone: marry, and be a Christian."[1] Dietrich Bonhoeffer said it more bluntly, "*Let him who cannot be alone beware of community. . . . Let him who is not in community beware of being alone.*"[2] We need both individual introspection and koinonia sharing for a full appreciation of what it means to live in the Cycle of Grace. So you are invited to share your experience of the Cycle of Grace with at least one other person.

Gathering a Group

Who will be part of your group? Whether two, three, six, or eight, your group can be a source of delight or a challenge to the spirit! While common practice is to post a note in the church newsletter and then to wait and see who shows up, a more proactive approach is to recruit a small group of people you perceive to be receptive to this material. Give yourself permission to identify your preferences for those who will accompany you on this journey. Whom do you want to be with? Whom do you want to get to know better? Whom do you feel you can trust? Remember that you and just one other person can count as a "small group," though the typical size is six to eight people.

Begin by reviewing the material in this book. *The Cycle of Grace* was developed specifically for busy, stressed leaders and pastors in today's church. The rich themes of Acceptance, Sustenance, Significance, and Fruitfulness touch the core of how Christ-followers are called to live today. Often as leaders we go the wrong way round by laboring hard (sometimes with bitterness) to bring in the kingdom, as though that was our job. For this reason, church leaders who feel they are too busy to attend may be exactly the people who need to participate. However, take note that if too many group members feel burned out, you may have difficulty moving beyond the negativity.

You may think of this as a one-on-one resource to share with your spiritual director, with a friend, with a small group of friends, or with the church's staff or leadership circle. Appendix D is included specifically for clergy groups, since that's the constituency that we worked with in Companions in Ministry. In whatever way you decide to share this material, we pray that the Cycle of Grace will bring or restore spiritual vitality to the circle of leaders who are so essential for the church's health.

Regardless of group size, read and refer regularly to the Guidelines for Sharing (Appendix B, page 103). Following these behavioral guidelines will allow for a healthy group experience. Ask everyone to be present and on time for all six sessions. Allow ninety minutes for each session (two hours to two-and-a-half hours for session two), keeping the group on schedule even when the conversation seems to go on and on. Use your judgment as to how to pace the group through the material; if you need more time on some parts, delete or shorten other sections as seems appropriate. Remind one another that consistent attendance helps to build trust, an essential ingredient for a good group experience.

A Gracious Space

Regardless of group size (two or more), spend time preparing spiritually and practically for the first meeting. Where will the group meet? Gathering in a home has advantages, providing there aren't too many distractions. If you decide to meet at the church, see if you can find a quiet room with a small, central table to serve as a worship center. Use visually pleasing cloths and a candle. Arrange for Taizé music or other gentle Christian songs to be playing as you gather. Think of each session as a mini-retreat. A retreat center in your area might have space to host the group meeting, though that may entail a fee. Watch the video segment at the beginning of the session. Bring paper, pens, name tags (if needed), and an extra copy or two of *The Cycle of Grace: Living in Sacred Balance* for anyone who needs one. Spend some time thinking about each of the participants. Make a few notes about what they said when you talked to them. Imagine what they may be feeling as they come to this first meeting. Say a prayer for them and for yourself as you guide the process and the group experience.

Throughout these sessions, we draw on the rich resources of the *Upper Room Worshipbook: Music and Liturgies for Spiritual Formation* (Upper Room Books, 2006). Hymns and songs were selected carefully to fit the theme for each session. Only the words are printed in this book, however, so you may want to obtain a copy of the *Worshipbook* for the music. An accompaniment book is also available through The Upper Room.

All sessions are ninety minutes long, except session two, which includes a meal. If you are preparing a meal together, plan on two and a half hours; if you are sharing a covered dish, plan on two hours.

SESSION ONE

Burnout, Jesus, and Grace

Materials needed: small table, candle, matches or lighter (for all sessions); paper, pens, name tags; bowl, pitcher of water, newsprint and markers

GATHER (10 MINUTES)

Welcome people, provide name tags if needed, and allow a few minutes for the group to gather. When you are ready, invite people to be seated in a circle with a candle and an empty bowl in the center of the circle on a small table. Light the candle, and invite them into a few minutes of silence as you gather in the presence of God. Then lead them in this or other opening.

> Leader: The grace of the Lord Jesus Christ be with you!
> Response: **And also with you!**
> Leader: The Risen Christ is with us!
> Response: **Thanks be to God!**

Say or sing "Water of Life" (URWB #422)

> **Water of life, Jesus our light; journey from death to new life. (2 times)**
> **Merciful God, gather us in; center us now in your grace. Fountain of love,**
> **source of all gifts; make us your people of peace.**

WORDS: David Haas ©1987 GIA Publications. Used by permission.

After a few moments, invite the participants to share a few words regarding their thoughts and feelings as they came, as well as their hopes for the group. Include your own thoughts about the value of this kind of group and then refer them to the "Guidelines for Sharing" (Appendix B, page 103). Invite their comments on each bullet point, and welcome further suggestions.

WATCH VIDEO (10 MINUTES)

Watch the video for session one (Acceptance). Give the group members time to ask questions or to make brief comments.

REVIEW AND DISCUSS (20 MINUTES)

Invite participants to choose a partner and share whatever they'd like from their journal for chapter one. After ten minutes, call the group back together in a circle. Invite people to ponder the question: **What are we learning about Acceptance?** Add your own insights to the conversation, and welcome their thoughts about this important topic. Allow at least ten minutes for this conversation.

ENGAGE AND REFLECT (40 MINUTES)

Note: Print the following words on newsprint for use at the close of this section:

"_____, you are beloved, a precious child of God, and beautiful to behold!"

Ask the group members to continue their consideration of Acceptance as they listen to a story by Janet Wolf titled "Chosen For . . . " You may wish to read the story or have someone else in the group read this story.

> In a world that pronounces so many of us "not good enough": what might it mean to believe that we really are chosen, precious, and beloved? In a new members' class we talked about baptism: this holy moment when we are named by God's grace with such power it won't come undone.
>
> Fayette was there—a woman living on the streets, struggling with mental illness and lupus. She loved the part about baptism and would ask over and over, "And when I'm baptized, I am . . . ?" We soon learned to respond, "Beloved, precious child of God, and beautiful to behold." "Oh, yes!" she'd say, and then we could go back to our discussion.
>
> The big day came. Fayette went under, came up spluttering, and cried, "And now I am . . . ?" And we all sang, "Beloved, precious child of God and beautiful to behold." "Oh, yes!" she shouted as she danced all around the fellowship hall.
>
> Two months later I got a call. Fayette had been beaten and raped and was at the county hospital. So I went. I could see her from a distance, pacing back and forth. When I got to the door, I heard, "I am beloved . . . " She turned, saw me, and said, "I am beloved, precious child of God, and . . . " Catching sight of herself in the mirror—hair sticking up, blood and tears streaking her face, dress torn, dirty, and rebuttoned askew, she started again, "I am beloved, precious child of God, and . . . " She looked in the mirror again and declared, " . . . and God is still working on me. If you come back tomorrow, I'll be so beautiful I'll take your breath away!"[3]

After the story has been read, ask participants to share aloud their thoughts related to Acceptance. Then tell the group members that you will be inviting them to reaffirm their baptism. If a participant has not been baptized, encourage him or her to think of this as a time of blessing for life. You may also want to invite the person to speak with the pastor about being baptized. Using the candle and bowl in the center of the circle, fill the bowl with water and bid people to remember their baptism. You may want to read the "Thanksgiving Over the Water" prayer from *The United Methodist Hymnal* (page 36) or a baptismal prayer from another tradition—or simply invite people to remember water as a sign of God's blessing. Then suggest that participants dip their fingers in the water to reaffirm God's blessing and to celebrate the grace freely bestowed on them in the Beloved. Then propose that each participant turn to the persons on either side of him or her (one at a time), take the wet hands, and quietly proclaim God's blessing with the words from the reading: "_____, **you are beloved, a precious child of God, and beautiful to behold!**" [printed on newsprint] Close this time with prayer.

BLESS AND CLOSE (10 MINUTES)

Ask the group to stay for a few minutes after the closing song to discuss session two. Read the following quotation from noted spiritual writer and author Henri J. M. Nouwen as a way to close this session.

> **Spiritual life starts at the place where you can hear God's voice. Where somehow you can claim that long before your father, your mother, your brother, your sister, your school, your church touched you, loved you, and wounded you—long before that, you were held safe in an eternal embrace. You were seen with eyes of perfect love long before you entered the dark valley of life. . . . The spiritual life starts at the moment you can go beyond all the wounds and claim that there was a love that was perfect and unlimited, long before that perfect love became reflected in the imperfect and limited, conditional love of people. The spiritual life begins where you dare to claim the first love—"Love one another because I have loved you first" (1 John 4:19).[4]**

With these words or in your own words, include the following thoughts:

> **We have focused this session on Acceptance and included the powerful experience of reaffirming our baptism and blessing. As we have focused on our own belovedness, we may have thought of others who need this love. As we close with prayer, you're invited to say the name of someone out loud without comment or silently in your heart. Then we'll join in the Lord's Prayer and close with a song.**

After the Lord's Prayer, sing or say "Bring Us Home" (URWB #61). Ask the group to stay for a few minutes before departure.

Chorus: **Bring us home on love's renewing tide to the place of our belonging. Bring us home to your redeeming side. Bring your scattered people home.**

Stanza 1: **From our weary night bring us to the light, to the place of our belonging; with your warm embrace, waken us to grace, bring your scattered people home.**

Stanza 2: **From our closed-in fears, from our wasted years, to the place of our belonging; to our highest call, sharing love with all, bring your scattered people home.**

Stanza 3: **From our selfish views, learnings we refuse, to the place of our belonging; to the truth we are, to our rising star, bring your scattered people home.**

Words © Rodney Romney; used by permission of Beverly Romney.

After singing, remind the participants to read chapter two and to respond to the Journaling Suggestions for the next meeting. Let them know they have two options: either prepare and share a meal together or bring a covered dish (potluck). Either option will involve adjusting the schedule; plan on at least two hours for covered dish and two and a half if preparing a meal. If the group decides to prepare a meal together, someone will need to shop for the ingredients and gather contributions to cover the cost.

SESSION TWO

Sustaining Grace

Materials needed: Bible for each participant and several Bible concordances; bowl and small loaf of bread; newsprint and markers

Remember for this session the group chose between two options: (1) a covered dish potluck; or (2) preparing and enjoying a meal together. You may need to remind people prior to the group meeting of the adjusted schedule.

GATHER (60 TO 90 MINUTES)

Welcome people as they arrive and proceed with the meal. Regardless of setting, let this be a time of relaxed and informal hospitality. Rather than fine china, use paper plates so no one has to labor long in the kitchen afterward. After the blessing, invite people to share a story about food or about a particularly notable meal they experienced, perhaps from childhood or young adult years. When the table has been cleared away, gather in the circle as you did last week. Place on the table a candle, the bowl from last week's baptismal renewal, and a small loaf of bread to symbolize the meal you've just shared. Light the candle, and invite people to sit in silence. Then share in the opening and song from last week.

> Leader: The grace of the Lord Jesus Christ be with you!
> Response: **And also with you!**
> Leader: The Risen Christ is with us!
> Response: **Thanks be to God!**

Say or sing "Water of Life" (URWB #422)

> **Water of life, Jesus our light; journey from death to new life. (2 times)**
> **Merciful God, gather us in; center us now in your grace. Fountain of love,**
> **source of all gifts; make us your people of peace.**

WORDS: David Haas ©1987 GIA Publications. Used by permission.

WATCH VIDEO (10 MINUTES)

Watch the second video segment (Sustenance). Allow time for brief discussion afterward.

REVIEW AND DISCUSS (20 MINUTES)

Invite participants to choose a different partner to share whatever they'd like from their journals (10 minutes). Gather the group again and ask the following: **What are we**

learning about Sustaining Grace? Incorporate insights from the corresponding chapter in this book.

Engage and Reflect (25 minutes)

For this portion of session two, participants need their Bibles and Bible concordances (or phone with Bible app). The group has been learning about sustaining grace and about the various ways Jesus sustained an intimate relationship with Abba. Together you have enjoyed a meal and experienced the importance of food and "table fellowship." Jesus often gathered with others around the table not just for food but also for teaching, for conversation, and for surprising acts of forgiveness and acceptance (such as Luke 7:36 and following). Long before the Last Supper, eating with Jesus must have been a profound experience!

Invite the group to learn more about table fellowship with Jesus by reviewing the Gospels. First list (on newsprint) as many stories as participants recall from memory, then add additional passages by paging through the Gospels or doing a word search in a concordance or on a phone app. Next select four or five passages to explore more thoroughly. Read the passage individually or in pairs and talk about what it says about "sustaining grace."

A list of passages can be quite long. The word *bread*, for example, appears fifty-eight times in the Gospels in the NRSV. Other words to search might include *meal, table, eat, dinner,* and *supper.* Sometimes scripture implies a meal, as when Jesus asks to "stay" at Zacchaeus's house (Luke 18). No wonder Jesus was accused of being a glutton and a drunkard (Matt. 11:19)!

Be sure to include the wedding feast; the feeding of the five thousand; the anticipated feast in the kingdom (Luke 13:29); as well as the meals with the Risen Lord. Quite a list! Ask the group, **What do these stories tell us about God's desire to sustain us?** The many stories and references to food suggest that God has a keen interest in sustaining us. The image of God as one who feeds us differs greatly from the notion of a distant, impersonal Being who pronounces judgment from on high. Spend some time talking about these ideas, noting in particular the variety of ways participants perceive God's image.

If the group members have not already made the connection to the sacrament of Holy Communion, invite them to do so. Knowing that Jesus often ate with the disciples may be new information for some people. Viewed in this context, the sacrament may be seen as the sustaining grace of a loving God who wants to keep us close.

Additional input you may wish to share and discuss:

John Wesley, founder of the Methodist movement, believed that God provided "The Means of Grace" by which we who seek to follow Christ might be sustained. In his sermon "Means of Grace" he lists three essential practices: "prayer, whether in secret or with the great congregation; searching the Scriptures (which implies

reading, hearing, and meditating thereon); and receiving the Lord's Supper, eating bread and drinking wine in remembrance of Him."[5]

It may surprise you to learn that Wesley, an activist in the faith, believed that it was just as important to be on the receiving end in the spiritual life as it was to give. While his list of spiritual practices may sound obvious, Wesley practiced what he preached as we can tell by the enthusiastic way he talked about each of them. In one of his sermons he wrote about "The Duty of Constant Communion." Here's an excerpt:

> The grace of God given herein [in receiving the Lord's Supper] confirms to us the pardon of our sins, by enabling us to leave them. As our bodies are strengthened by bread and wine, so are our souls by these tokens of the body and blood of Christ. This is the food of our souls: This gives strength to perform our duty, and leads us on to perfection. If, therefore, we have any regard for the plain command of Christ, if we desire the pardon of our sins, if we wish for strength to believe, to love and obey God, then we should neglect no opportunity of receiving the Lord's Supper; then we must never turn our backs on the feast which our Lord has prepared for us.[6]

Bless and Close (5 minutes)

Sing or say together "For Your Generous Providing" (URWB #82) to the tune of "Holy Manna" or "Hymn to Joy."

For your generous providing which sustains us all our days,
for your Spirit here residing, we proclaim our heartfelt praise.
Through the depths of joy and sorrow, though the road be smooth or rough,
fearless, we can face tomorrow for your grace will be enough.

Hush our world's seductive voices tempting us to stand alone;
save us, then, from siren noises calling us to trust our own.
For those snared by earthly treasure, lured by false security,
Jesus, true and only measure, spring the trap to set folk free.

'Round your table, through your giving, show us how to live and pray
till your kingdom's way of living is the bread we share each day:
Bread for us and for our neighbor; bread for body, mind, and soul,
bread of heav'n and human labor—broken bread that makes us whole.

—Used by permission of the Mission and Discipleship Council, The Church of Scotland

Join together in the Lord's Prayer and close with this blessing from Ephesians 3:20-21 (or another benediction of your choice):

> Now to him who by the power at work within us is able to accomplish abundantly far more than all we can ask or imagine, to him be glory in the church and in Christ Jesus to all generations, forever and ever. Amen.

SESSION THREE

You Are a Sign

Materials needed: broken loaf from previous session, a collection of photographs for the "Engage and Reflect" exercise

(Refer to that section now for suggestions about the type of photographs and where to find them.)

GATHER (5 MINUTES)

Welcome participants to the circle, with candle, bowl and bread in the center. When all are comfortable, light the candle and share in an extended period of silence, noticing how much more comfortable you are as a group in this your third session. Join in the opening response and song as per session one.

> Leader: The grace of the Lord Jesus Christ be with you!
> Response: **And also with you!**
> Leader: The Risen Christ is with us!
> Response: **Thanks be to God!**

Say or sing "Water of Life" (URWB #422)

> **Water of life, Jesus our light; journey from death to new life. (2 times)**
> **Merciful God, gather us in; center us now in your grace. Fountain of love,**
> **source of all gifts; make us your people of peace.**

WORDS: David Haas ©1987 GIA Publications. Used by permission.

Before you watch the video, review the "Guidelines for Sharing" (Appendix B, page 103) that you introduced during session one. Invite comments and encourage one another in creating a sense of trust and openness to God.

WATCH VIDEO (10 MINUTES)

Watch the third video segment ("Significance"). Allow time for a short discussion afterward about the meaning of the word *significance* before moving on.

REVIEW AND DISCUSS (20 MINUTES)

Invite participants to choose a different partner to share whatever they'd like from their journals (10 minutes). Gather the group again and ask the following: **What are we learning about what it means to be a sign of God's grace?** Incorporate insights from the corresponding chapter in this book into your conversation.

ENGAGE AND REFLECT (50 MINUTES)

This exercise requires a variety of photographs: trees, people, animals, plants, landscapes—both abstract and realistic. Its purpose is to encourage people to look deeply and not just glance at the world and its immense wonders. For three or four people, twenty or thirty photographs will suffice; for eight to ten people, you'll need fifty. You can build a collection by looking through magazines, developing your own pictures, or by going to the website at GBOD Sight Psalms http://www.gbod.org/site/c.nhLRJ2PMKsG/b.6174501/k.9236/Sight_Psalms.htm. Scatter the pictures on a table, and give the following instructions. Invite the group members to come to the table in silence and to remain silent as they view the photographs. Encourage them to take the necessary time to find the photo that best speaks to their spiritual life. Participants may find that a picture chooses them, intriguing them in ways that they don't immediately understand! As each person makes a mental selection, he or she returns to a seat and waits until all have returned to their seats. When all are seated, ask the participants to retrieve their picture from the table and return with it to their chairs. If two or more persons have selected the same photograph, they can either select a second choice or share it with the other persons. When everyone is seated and photograph in hand or nearby, invite each person to state aloud the perceived connection of the picture to his or her spiritual life.

Note: Participants often express surprise about the power of this exercise. Visual images speak to the human soul in surprising ways. All of life is a sign of God if one has eyes to see. Each of us is called to be a sign of God's grace in our own unique and powerful way.

After the picture exercise you may want to take a short break before reconvening. Introduce the story below as follows:

> **Shirley Montoya, a United Methodist pastor from a Navajo tribe in Arizona, wrote the following meditation for *Alive Now*. Her story suggests that every created thing, including an oak tree in the high desert, shimmers with the presence of God if we have eyes to see. When we take time to look, we may gain insights as to how we are called to be a sign of God's presence in the world.**

Read or have someone read "The Spirit Tree" by Shirley C. Montoya from *Alive Now* May/June 2007:

> **Upon entering the Diné [dih-NAY] (Navajo) reservation where I was born and reared, I am hit with the stark reality that this nation is isolated and insulated. Yet, the societal issues and problems are not unlike the rest of the world. The Nation is caught making its way between worlds: Western European and traditional Diné cultures, caught between two different rhythms in the seasons of life.**

There are days I simply want to stay under the warmth and safety of my comforter listening to the world murmuring or buzzing outside without my input. There are days when I feel the weight of the day before I even set foot into the world, but smelling the coffee my husband, Robert, is brewing and knowing that my cup will soon arrive is an enticement to rise and shine.

Opportunities abound. One morning, I notice an oak tree standing in front of the clinic. I pick up some fallen leaves and notice that no two leaves are alike and the colors are of many shades: gold, yellow, green, brown and red. The huge, towering tree lifts its many arms toward the sky. Surely the strength of this oak tree was not grown overnight. It took many years of nurture, water, sunlight, and care.

When I look up into the tree again, it seems to pray:

By your Holy Spirit, I am tall and strong with many arms and leaves of many shapes and colors. I lift my arms in celebration to receive your holy light. I provide shelter for your people and creation.

By your Holy Spirit, I provide music for all to hear, stirred by the warm summer breezes and through the whipping of the harsh winter blizzards. I provide a sense of endurance and stability for those who become weak, confused and in need of affirmation. I provide a beauty for all to see anytime and anywhere.

By your Holy Spirit, I grow with the seasons and see leaves and arms fall with the years, and as I begin to die, I am comforted to know that I am loved by the one who planted me and the one who nurtured me.

By your Holy Spirit, I provide a testament of your creative hands and presence. I provide a commitment to ensure that every part of me is given the opportunity to grow to its fullest beauty. I am God's creation. I am shelter. I am beauty. I am love. I am the Spirit Tree.[7]

Invite participants' response to the story before moving on.

Bless and Close (5 minutes)

Say or sing together "Loving Spirit" (URWB #203). The words may be sung to the tune of "Faith, While Trees Are Still in Blossom" (UMH #508).

Loving Spirit, loving Spirit,
   you have chosen me to be—
   you have drawn me to your wonder,
you have set your sign on me.

Like a mother you enfold me,
   hold my life within your own,
   feed me with your very body,
form me of your flesh and bone.

Like a father you protect me,
    teach me the discerning eye,
    hoist me up upon your shoulder,
let me see the world from high.

Friend and lover, in your closeness
    I am known and held and blessed:
    In your promise is your comfort,
in your presence I may rest.

Loving Spirit, loving Spirit,
    you have chosen me to be—
    you have drawn me to your wonder,
you have set your sign on me.

Close with last session's benediction from Ephesians 3:20-21 (or another benediction of your choice):

Now to him who by the power at work within us is able to accomplish abundantly far more than all we can ask or imagine, to him be glory in the church and in Christ Jesus to all generations, forever and ever. Amen.

SESSION FOUR

Fruitfulness and the Cycle of Works

Materials needed: unlined paper; colored pens, pencils, or markers; Bible for each participant

GATHER (5 MINUTES)

Welcome participants to the circle with candle, bowl and bread in the center. Include also one or more of the pictures from the last session to build continuity from the last session. When everyone is seated, light the candle and share in the silence. Join in the opening response and song as per session one.

> Leader: The grace of the Lord Jesus Christ be with you!
> Response: **And also with you!**
> Leader: The Risen Christ is with us!
> Response: **Thanks be to God!**

Say or sing "Water of Life" (URWB #422)

> **Water of life, Jesus our light; journey from death to new life. (2 times)**
> **Merciful God, gather us in; center us now in your grace. Fountain of love,**
> **source of all gifts; make us your people of peace.**

WORDS: David Haas ©1987 GIA Publications. Used by permission.

WATCH VIDEO (10 MINUTES)

Watch the fourth video segment (Fruitfulness). Allow time for a brief discussion of the video, and then move on.

REVIEW AND DISCUSS (30 MINUTES)

Invite participants to pair up and share from their reading and from their journals (10 minutes). Gather the group again, and ask the following questions: **What is the difference between living in the Cycle of Grace and living (or surviving) in the Cycle of Works? What have you observed in others? What have you observed in yourself?**

ENGAGE AND REFLECT (40 MINUTES)

Remind participants that the Bible contains many images that suggest the difference between a God-centered life and a life that has departed from God's way. For example, in

Isaiah 5, the prophet confronts Israel's unfaithfulness, which results in "wild grapes" too small and bitter for wine. We find another example in Psalm 1. Read aloud the following:

> **Psalm 1 offers a stark contrast between those who are securely planted in God's Torah and those who are not. The word *Torah* here may be better translated as "way" rather than "law"; indeed, it was God's life-giving way that the ancient Hebrew writer envisioned. The Torah embodied a dynamic reality rather than a rigid code to be slavishly followed.**

Ask a volunteer to read Psalm 1 aloud. Then ask the participants to take a sheet of paper and colored markers, pens, or pencils and sketch out the contrasting images from this psalm. Invite them to use their imagination as they respond to the scripture. Encourage them to bring insights from the four movements in the Cycle of Grace: Acceptance, Sustenance, Significance, and Fruitfulness. What does a Cycle of Works tree look like?

When the group members have finished their drawings, invite them to share sketches and insights they have gained about these two different ways of living.

Then read aloud to the group the following Simone Weil quotation:

> **It is the light continuously falling from heaven which alone gives a tree the energy to send powerful roots deep into the earth. The tree is really rooted in the sky.**[8]

Bless and Close (5 minutes)

Say or sing "Psalm 1" (Happy Are They) URWB #223 using Refrain 2.

Refrain 2: **"Like a tree that's planted by the water, we shall not be moved."**

Stanzas 1 and 2:

Happy indeed are they who refuse the way of the evil; nor walk the road of the sinners, or join the mockers of God.

Joy shall be in the hearts of those who delight in the Word of God; for they consume that Word, consume it day and night.

Repeat Refrain 2

Stanzas 3 and 4:

They are like green trees that grow by clear flowing waters, they bear their fruit in due season, their leaves fade not, they prosper.

Thus it is not so, not so with evil doers, they blow like chaff in the wind, they fall by weight of the Truth.

Repeat Refrain 2

Stanza 5:

God upholds the just, God knows the way of the righteous, but the evil ones shall perish, they perish by their deeds.

Repeat Refrain 2

Close this session with the Lord's Prayer and the benediction from Ephesians 3:20-21 (or another benediction of your choice):

> **Now to him who by the power at work within us is able to accomplish abundantly far more than all we can ask or imagine, to him be glory in the church and in Christ Jesus to all generations, forever and ever. Amen.**

SESSION FIVE

A Grace-Filled Way to Live

Materials needed: creation photo and drawing from last session

GATHER (5 MINUTES)

Welcome participants to the circle with candle, bowl, bread and a photograph from session three in the center. Include also one or more of the drawings from session four or perhaps a copy of Psalm 1. When everyone is seated, light the candle and share in the silence. Join in the opening response and song as noted in session one.

> Leader: The grace of the Lord Jesus Christ be with you!
> Response: **And also with you!**
> Leader: The Risen Christ is with us!
> Response: **Thanks be to God!**

Say or sing "Water of Life" (URWB #422)

> **Water of life, Jesus our light; journey from death to new life. (2 times)**
> **Merciful God, gather us in; center us now in your grace. Fountain of love,**
> **source of all gifts; make us your people of peace.**

WORDS: David Haas ©1987 GIA Publications. Used by permission.

WATCH VIDEO (10 MINUTES)

Watch the fifth video segment (A Grace-Filled Way to Live). Note that the video includes comments about the rule of life, the focus for this session, as well as comments about Congregational Vitality, the topic for the next session.

REVIEW AND DISCUSS (20 MINUTES)

Invite participants to choose a different partner to share whatever they'd like from their journals (10 minutes). Then encourage the pairs to discuss their answers to the question, **What am I learning about a grace-filled way to live?** After ten minutes, bring the group together to share responses to this question.

ENGAGE AND REFLECT (45 MINUTES)

Ask participants to review what they have recorded as their rule of life. If they have not yet written anything, give them some time to do so, using their response to the Journaling Suggestions as a guide. When they are ready, invite them to share what they have written with the group. As each person shares, the other participants are encouraged to listen in an open, prayerful way without judgment or advice. As each person finishes speaking, sing or say "Take, O Take Me As I Am" (below). Sit in silence for a few moments before moving on to the next person. Remind the participants that a rule of life is like a trellis; it is meant to provide support and growth, not a sense of failure.

BLESS AND CLOSE (10 MINUTES)

When all have shared, read "A Blessing" (URWB #112) slowly out loud. You may want to have a different person read each paragraph:

> I pray that Christ may come to you early in the morning, as he came to Mary that morning in the garden. And I pray that you find Christ in the night when you need him as Nicodemus did. May Christ come to you while you are a child, for when disciples tried to stop them, Jesus insisted that the children come to him.
>
> I pray that Christ may come to you when you are old, as he came to old Simeon's arms and made him cry: "Lord, now let your servant depart in peace, for my eyes have seen your salvation."
>
> And may Christ come to you in your grief as he did for Mary and Martha when they lost their brother. May Christ come to you in joy as he did to the wedding in Cana. And may Christ visit you when you are sick, as he did for the daughter of Jairus, and for so many who could not walk, or stand straight, or see, or hear till he came.
>
> May the Lord Jesus come in answer to your questions as he once did for a lawyer and a rich young ruler. And in your madness may he stand before you in all his power as he stood among the graves that day before Legion.
>
> May Christ come to you in glory upon your dying day as he did to the thief hanging beside him that Good Friday. And though you seldom come to him, and though you often "make your bed in hell," as I do, may you find Christ descending there, where the apostles in their creed agreed he went—so you would know there is no place he would not come for you.

© 2006 Chuck Wilhelm. Used by permission.

Say or sing: "Take, O Take Me As I Am" (URWB #441)

> Take, O take me as I am. Summon out what I shall be;
> set your seal upon my heart and live in me.

WORDS: John L. Bell ©1995 Wild Goose Resource Group, Iona Community, Scotland; GIA Publications, Inc., exclusive North American agent. Used by permission.

Close with prayer and an affirmation for what you as individuals and as a group are doing to live in the Cycle of Grace.

SESSION SIX

Congregational Vitality and the Cycle of Grace

Materials needed: a trellis or other symbol from previous session; elements for Holy Communion or a Love Feast, chalice and paten

GATHER (5 MINUTES)

Add a trellis or some other symbol from the last session as you gather around in a circle to share the opening ritual by lighting the candle, sitting in silence, and joining in the opening response and song as noted in session one.

> Leader: The grace of the Lord Jesus Christ be with you!
> Response: **And also with you!**
> Leader: The Risen Christ is with us!
> Response: **Thanks be to God!**

Say or sing "Water of Life" (URWB #422)

> **Water of life, Jesus our light; journey from death to new life. (2 times)**
> **Merciful God, gather us in; center us now in your grace. Fountain of love,**
> **source of all gifts; make us your people of peace.**

WATCH VIDEO (0 MINUTES)

Session six has no video component. The session five video briefly referred to congregational vitality, the topic for this session.

REVIEW AND DISCUSS (30 MINUTES)

Invite participants to choose a partner and share their responses to the Journaling Suggestions for Days One, Two, Three, and Four. The Journaling Suggestions for these four days correspond to the movements in the Cycle of Grace: Acceptance, Sustenance, Significance, and Fruitfulness. As participants reflect on how their congregation embodies each of these elements, they are encouraged to grow in their attentiveness to God's presence among them. When ready, bring the group together and invite them to respond to the questions, **How does the Cycle of Grace help me to see God's grace at work in our congregation more clearly? How can we expand our attentiveness to God's presence in our midst?**

Engage and Reflect (30 minutes)

When the group members are ready to move on, invite them to listen to the following story from *Alive Now*. The story, titled "Bonded," was written by Gary Kennedy, pastor of a congregation in Arizona.[9]

> A few years ago David, a young leader in our congregation, asked for prayers for his family, who were in the midst of a trying time related to his need for a kidney transplant and failure to find an eligible donor. Unknown to anyone in David's family, the prayer request inspired several persons in the church to investigate whether they could be suitable donors. As a result, Lori came forward stating that she was a match and was willing to give a kidney to David. Lori did not know David personally but had heard of his plight in church. She and her husband, Stuart, believed that Christians are called to unity, even with those we do not know; they were moved to try to help.
>
> In an emotionally and spiritually charged service, the congregation prayed for Lori and David the Sunday before the surgeries. Everyone in the congregation got up at 5:00 a.m. the day of the transplant to pray for both of them. The transplant was a success, and the two families are now bonded by the experience. More than that, the congregation is now more profoundly bonded to a God who helps us know we are all called to be one with each other in the wonderful mystery that is the church.
>
> The power of the sacramental prayer* is the miracle of the church in action, which happens when people embrace their call as individuals and then collectively respond in working together through the church to live out that call. Genuine excitement ripples from individuals to a congregation, to the larger church, to the world each time a person takes hold of his or her call and responds unselfishly.

*The sacramental prayer referred to here is this: "By your Spirit make us one with Christ, one with each other, and one in ministry to all the world" (UMH, 10).

Invite the group to respond to this story using the following questions:

- In your opinion, how does the story suggest that this congregation was living in the Cycle of Grace? What movement in the Cycle is represented (Acceptance, Sustenance, Significance, or Fruitfulness)?
- Many people today are dropping out of congregational life, preferring to take an individualized approach to life's challenges. What does the story say about that trend?
- What changes in the story would have made it more powerful for you?
- How does the story challenge efforts to measure congregational vitality based solely on numbers (membership, finances, attendance)?

BLESS AND CLOSE (25 MINUTES)

If an ordained clergyperson is a part of the group, you may wish to close with the sacrament of Holy Communion. If Communion is not an option, you may want to close with a Love Feast, or Agape Meal. See *The United Methodist Book of Worship* (pages 581–84) for guidelines. Include the song "Vine and Branches" (URWB #107).

Stanza 1: You are the vine and we are your branches, one with your life, and rooted in your heart. Flowing with grace, with life you fill us, strengthened that nothing can break us apart.

Stanza 2: You are the vine and we are your branches, flowing with power greater than our own. You grant us grace to love each other. Yours are the fruits that within us have grown.

Stanza 3: You are the vine and we are your branches, One common blood flows through all of our veins. We all are part of one another. We are all branches of one living vine.

Stanza 4: You are the vine and we are your branches, Deep in our hearts your life is flowing through. Rooted in you, we grow and flourish. You live within us, and we live in you.

Words and Music: © 2005 Steve Garnaas-Holmes. Used by permission.

Close with the benediction from Ephesians 3:20-21 (or another benediction of your choice):

> Now to him who by the power at work within us is able to accomplish abundantly far more than all we can ask or imagine, to him be glory in the church and in Christ Jesus to all generations, forever and ever. Amen.

Notes

ONE: BURNOUT, JESUS, AND GRACE

1. Frank Lake sought to develop a model for theology and psychodynamic theory that correlated "the biblical material concerning Christ . . . with the sum of our knowledge of human personality growth and development" [*Clinical Theology: A Theological and Psychological Basis to Clinical Pastoral Care*, abridged by Martin H. Yeomans (London: Darton, Longman & Todd, 1986) 29]. While much theology focused on sin and much psychiatry focused on sickness, Lake believed a model reflecting the dynamics of well-functioning personality and spiritual health was needed. Reviewing the work of Freud, Adler and Jung, Lake realized every theorist made a choice, "*an act of faith*" [his italics] as to who represented the norm for humanity. Lake based his model on Christ and called it "The Dynamic Cycle" (35–36). Followers of Frank Lake changed the name of the model to the Cycle of Grace, which is the term used in this book.

2. Ibid, 29.

3. Marian Cowan, "How Ignatius Would Tend the Holy: Ignatian Spirituality and Spiritual Direction," in *Tending the Holy: Spiritual Direction across Tradition*, ed. Norvene Vest (Harrisburg, PA: Morehouse Publishing, 2003), 74.

4. Ibid.

5. John Allen, *Rabble-Rouser for Peace: The Authorized Biography of Desmond Tutu* (New York, London, Toronto, Sydney: Free Press, 2006), 307.

TWO: SUSTAINING GRACE

1. Jean Vanier, *Drawn into the Mystery of Jesus through the Gospel of John* (Paulist Press: New York/Mahwah, NJ, 2003), 195ff.

2. Lisa A. Myers, "From a Graceful Center: Spiritual Directions for Evangelicals," in *Tending the Holy: Spiritual Direction across Tradition*, ed. Norvene Vest (Harrisburg, PA: Morehouse Publishing, 2003), 87.

3. Ibid, 88.

4. Ibid, 89.

5. John Wesley, Sermon 89, "The More Excellent Way," http://umcmission.org/Find-Resources/Global-Worship-and-Spiritual-Growth/John-Wesley-Sermons/Sermon-89-The-More-Excellent-Way. See also John Wesley, Sermon 93, "On Redeeming the Time," http://umcmission.org/Find-Resources/Global-Worship-and Spiritual-Growth/John-Wesley-Sermons/Sermon-93-On-Redeeming-The-Time.

THREE: YOU ARE A SIGN

1. Lake used the term *Status* rather than *Significance*. [*Clinical Theology*, 29]. This word fits with the theology of the Gospel of John, where Jesus' real status as the Son of God becomes more

and more apparent to his followers. Students of Frank Lake preferred the term *Significance*, which avoids the implications of class and hierarchy.

2. E. Glenn Hinson, *Love at the Heart of Things: A Biography of Douglas V. Steere* (Wallingford, PA: Pendle Hill Publications, 1998), 1.

3. Kenda Creasy Dean and Ron Foster. *The Godbearing Life: The Art of Soul Tending for Youth Ministry* (Nashville, TN: Upper Room Books, 1998), 52.

4. Ibid.

5. Herbert Alphonso, S.J., *Discovering Your Personal Vocation: The Search for Meaning through the Spiritual Exercises* (New York/Mahwah, NJ: Paulist Press, 2001), 2.

6. Ibid, xii; from the Foreword by Dennis Linn, Sheila Fabricant Linn, Matthew Linn, S.J.

7. M. Robert Mulholland Jr., *Shaped by the Word: The Power of Scripture in Spiritual Formation*, rev. (Nashville, TN: Upper Room Books, 2000), 34.

8. Mother Teresa of Calcutta, quoted in *The Communion of Saints: Prayers of the Famous*, ed. Horton Davies (Grand Rapids, MI: William B. Eerdmans Publishing Company, 1990), 69.

FOUR: FRUITFULNESS AND THE CYCLE OF WORKS

1. Lake used the term *Achievement* for this fourth movement [*Clinical Theology*, 29]. Trevor prefers the term *Fruitfulness*, which lends itself to a more organic understanding of grace.

2. Anonymous. Used by permission.

3. Simone Weil, "Human Personality," in *Simone Weil: An Anthology*; ed. Siân Miles (New York: Weidenfeld & Nicolson, 1986), 66.

FIVE: A GRACE-FILLED WAY TO LIVE

1. Marjorie J. Thompson, *Soul Feast: An Invitation to the Christian Spiritual Life* (Louisville, KY: Westminster John Knox Press, 2005), 146.

2. Thornton Wilder, *Our Town: A Play in Three Acts* (New York: HarperCollins, 2003), 46.

3. L. Roger Owens, *Abba, Give Me a Word: The Path of Spiritual Direction* (Brewster, MA: Paraclete, 2012); see especially chapter 3, "Releasing," 47–71.

4. Mary Margaret Funk, *Tools Matter for Practicing the Spiritual Life* (London: Continuum, 2001), 2.

5. See *The Meeting [God] Bible: Growing in Intimacy with God through Scripture* (Nashville, TN: Upper Room Books, 1999, 2008).

6. John Allen, *Rabble-Rouser for Peace: The Authorized Biography of Desmond Tutu* (New York/ London/Toronto/Sydney: Free Press, 2006), 307.

7. Pope John XXIII, *Journal of a Soul*, trans. Dorothy White (New York: McGraw-Hill, 1964), 5.

SIX: CONGREGATIONAL VITALITY AND THE CYCLE OF GRACE

*Michel Bouttier, *Prayers for My Village*, trans. Lamar Williamson (Nashville, TN: Upper Room Books, 1994), 64.

1. In 2003 Jerry worked with John Doble and Associates Research Group of Summit, New Jersey, to assess the impact of The Academy for Spiritual Formation on clergy participants. With funding from the Lilly Endowment, the tools of social science were used for this

comprehensive twelve-month study. Under the guidance of the research group, founders and key leaders for this ministry answered a series of questions defining the method and goals of the Academy. After gaining a good understanding of the purpose of the Academy, the researchers then asked, "What is it that you don't know that you want to know?" Several conversations and much thought followed, finally producing a set of questions to be offered to a series of focus groups that met in different regions of the country. The focus-group sessions were recorded, and the recordings were analyzed thoroughly. Finally, a written survey was sent to the targeted audience. Results from the written survey were then tabulated with graphs and tables and considered "hard data." While the hard data is impressive, Jerry felt the real value of this process came in formulating precise questions and listening intently to the responses. The assessment seemed clear before the graphs and tables were published. This research is available by going to the Academy website: http://academy.upperroom.org/about/research

2. Bouttier, *Prayers for My Village*, 84.

SHARING THE JOURNEY AND SESSION OUTLINES

*Kieran Kavanaugh, *John of the Cross: Doctor of Light and Love*, The Crossroad Spiritual Legacy series (New York: Crossroad, 1999), 48.

1. Paul Tournier, *Escape from Loneliness*, trans. John S. Gilmour (Philadelphia, PA: The Westminster Press, 1962), 25.

2. Dietrich Bonhoeffer, *Life Together: The Classic Exploration of Christian Community* (New York: Harper One, 1954), 77.

3. From *The Upper Room Disciplines 1999* (Nashville, TN: Upper Room Books, 1998), 128.

4. Excerpt from a lecture delivered by Henri J. M. Nouwen, Scarritt-Bennett Center, Nashville, Tennessee; February 8, 1991.

5. John Wesley, Sermon 16, "The Means of Grace," http://new.gbgm-umc.org/umhistory/wesley/sermons/16/

6. John Wesley, Sermon 101, "The Duty of Constant Communion," http://new.gbgm-umc.org/umhistory/wesley/sermons/101/

7. Shirley C. Montoya, "The Spirit Tree," *Alive Now* (May/June 2007): 10, 12.

8. Weil, in *Simone Weil: An Anthology*, 66.

9. Gary Kennedy, "Bonded," *Alive Now* (May/June 2007): 42–43.

APPENDIX A

Summary of Video Segments

A summary of each video segment of *The Cycle of Grace: Living in Sacred Balance* is below for your convenience.

SESSION ONE

Introduction to *The Cycle of Grace* and the first movement in the Cycle—Acceptance—as described by the Rev. Trevor Hudson:

Dr. Frank Lake, a British psychologist, developed the concept of the Cycle of Grace in the 1950s and published it in his book *Clinical Theology*. I learned about it through one of Dr. Lake's former students, the Rev. Anne Long.

Dr. Lake's concern centered on how quickly missionaries to India became burned out. They left for their post, eager and enthusiastic, yet soon became resentful and cynical. As he continued to study the phenomenon, he came into contact with a Swiss theologian by the name of Emil Brunner. Together the two of them began reading and reflecting on the Gospel life of Jesus to see if they could detect some pattern that might explain why Jesus never seemed to burn out, even though he experienced enormous stress.

The first aspect that Lake and Brunner noticed was the sense of *balance* in Jesus' life. Jesus engaged in ministry in significant ways but also allowed time for renewal. In Mark 1:29-39 Jesus engages in exhausting ministry—healing, teaching, and casting out demons. Yet he takes time for personal renewal by withdrawing "to a lonely place" (v. 35, NIV) to pray. Lake and Brunner began to see a pattern that, for the uses of this study, is called the Cycle of Grace. [See the graph on the next page.]

At two places on the graph, grace flows *into* Jesus' life, indicated by the arrows. The first movement is an inflow of God's grace referred to as Acceptance. In Jesus' life, this inflow of grace occurs at his baptism when the Voice from heaven says, "You are my Son, my Beloved." Brunner and Lake believe this spiritual foundation lies at the heart of Jesus' ministry. From this point on, Jesus knows himself as beloved child of God. And with his identity intact, Jesus began his ministry.

Powerful words of Acceptance are spoken to Jesus at another moment in his life: On the mountain, before he enters Jerusalem, Jesus is transfigured and the words are again said, "This is my Beloved Son." God's gracious Acceptance empowers Jesus to face his suffering and death as he draws on the knowledge of God's unconditional love.

Based on this understanding of Jesus' life and ministry, Lake and Brunner felt it of chief importance for persons entering ministry to come to terms with their own story and to claim their identity as a child of God. Ministry begins with a deep knowledge of our Acceptance by God. That is the first movement in the Cycle of Grace.

Cycle of Grace

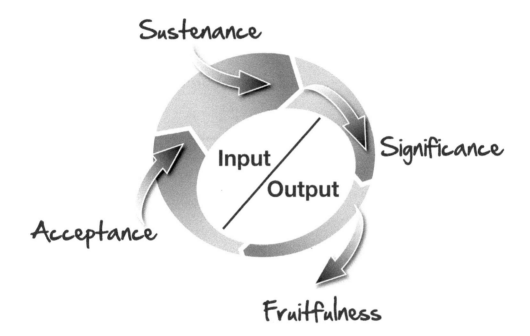

SESSION TWO

Review of session one, followed by a discussion of the second movement in the Cycle of Grace: Sustenance. Rev. Hudson discusses how Jesus sustained his relationship with Abba God and invites the participants to respond with their own insights.

The first segment introduced the Cycle of Grace and described the places of Acceptance in Jesus' life. Lake and Brunner acknowledged that these moments marked Jesus' life, and they further noted that Jesus built into his daily living a number of practices that sustained him. For this reason, the Cycle of Grace refers to this movement as Sustenance.

In what ways did Jesus sustain his close relationship with God throughout his life? What comes to mind?

1. Prayer—Jesus withdrew to places of silence and solitude at critical moments in his life.
2. A close circle of friends—Jesus had a rich relational life. He spent time with the disciples and maintained a special relationship with the three who accompanied him to the Mount of Transfiguration. He called John his "beloved disciple." Beyond the disciples, he often stayed with friends Mary, Martha, and Lazarus in Bethany and interacted with many others.
3. Breaking bread and spending time in fellowship—Jesus seemed to enjoy parties! The Gospels often depict him at table, and, at one point, his adversaries called him a glutton and a wine bibber. Jesus experienced joy and celebrated life.
4. Community worship—Jesus spent a great deal of time in the synagogue "as was his custom," even though the synagogue often brought trouble.
5. Time with scripture—Jesus immersed himself in the scriptures of his day, the Old Testament. The scriptures provided a source of strength; for example, during his desert temptations.

These five practices provided sustenance for Jesus' life. This book describes more. Notice how the Cycle of Grace becomes thicker here, suggesting that these practices strengthen Jesus for ministry. It's encouraging to realize that Jesus shared our humanity so fully that he needed such practices to sustain his relationship with God.

Session Three

Rev. Jerry Haas joins Rev. Hudson in a discussion of the third movement in the Cycle of Grace, Significance. While the first and second movements (Acceptance and Sustenance) represent the *input* of grace into our lives, this movement and the fourth movement show how grace flows through us in response to the world's needs.

After Trevor briefly introduced this session, Jerry went on to comment. The following is a paraphrase of their conversation.

> *Jerry:* "I'm fascinated with the word *significance* here. It seems to me to indicate that before we ask, 'What did Jesus do?' we need to ask, 'What did his life signify?' To signify is to be a sign for something, and Jesus never seemed to forget that his life was a sign for God's grace, just as we are also called to be such a sign."

> *Trevor* responded with these thoughts: "Yes, and when we think of the various 'I am' sayings in the Gospel: 'I am the bread of life,' 'I am the resurrection and the life,' 'I am the light of the world,' we hear him describing who he was and is. His identity and our own individual identities as human beings are gifts to the world.

> "I really think that every human being has a need for significance. We all want our lives to signify something, and that's part of our search. I recently led a course in which I asked the people to say something about their unique way of being in

the world, what they wanted their life to signify, and it was fascinating. One person talked about how he wanted to be a brother; another said 'a conversational partner,' another person said 'a revealer of goodness in all created things.' I think for me what I want is to be a companion, a friend to others.

"Bottom line: When we're gone, I believe people will remember what kind of person we are more than what we did."

Jerry: "Our lives are a gift from God; our individual lives are a gift from God. Part of the challenge of life is to discover what that individual gift is."

Trevor: "I heard a legend once that God sends each person into the world with a song to sing, a message to deliver, a special way to be in the world. Part of ministry is the offering of that gift."

Session Four

Rev. Hudson describes the fourth and final movement in the Cycle of Grace, *Fruitfulness*, a word he prefers to the original word *Achievement* used by Lake and Brunner. After drawing on the audience for ideas about the activities of Jesus' ministry, Trevor points out that the mission workers reversed the flow, creating a Cycle of Works instead of a Cycle of Grace, which resulted in burnout.

What are some examples of the way in which grace flowed out of Jesus' life to the world?

- Ministry with the children. Children felt valued when they were with Jesus despite living in a society that didn't value children.
- Transformation. Zacchaeus exemplifies a person transformed by his encounter with Jesus; so too is the woman caught in adultery.
- People on the margins. Jesus gave space to those who were told they didn't belong.
- Followers, those who defended him. Jesus' disciples were not only a source of sustenance; they became ministry teams that carried on his work in the world.

Trevor: "As we look at the Cycle of Grace now as a whole, remember why Brunner and Lake put it together. The mission workers were not living this way. They were burning themselves out. Instead of moving clockwise with the Cycle of Grace, they were moving counterclockwise, creating a Cycle of Works. They started out trying to be fruitful, so that they could be significant, hoping then to gain sustenance so that they might be accepted. This is really where the lights went on for me as I saw how easy it is to get caught in the Cycle of Works in the ministry. In many ways, our whole culture pulls us in this direction."

Cycle of Works

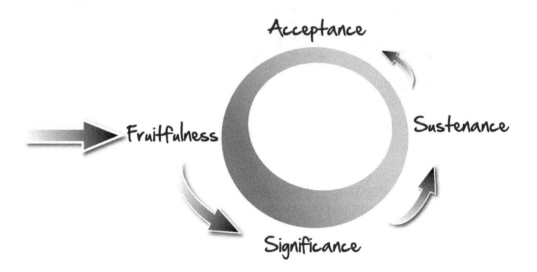

Acceptance

Fruitfulness

Sustenance

Significance

SESSION FIVE

In the final video session, Rev. Jerry Haas and Ms. Sarah Wilke join Rev. Hudson to discuss questions and implications raised by the model of the Cycle of Grace. The following is a paraphrase of their conversation.

> *Sarah*: "What I like about this model is how it images God's grace all the way through our lives. When I worked in inner-city ministry, I saw and felt the dynamics of burnout regularly."

> *Trevor*: "Besides looking at the Cycle of Grace as a model for our individual lives, we can also use it as a way of looking at our congregational life. For example, are there places in our congregation where people might experience Acceptance or are we too caught up in the need for results?

> *Jerry*: "When I learned about the Cycle of Grace, I thought of how helpful it is in shaping a rule of life, either for ourselves individually or for us as a congregation."

> *Sarah*: "Trevor, what about the notion that you need to engage people in ministry first as a strategy for church growth. Doesn't that sound like the Cycle of Works?"

> *Trevor*: "No, because people can enter the church's ministries at any point. The key is for people to move through the cycle. Otherwise, they may be desperately trying to create the acceptance that God has already given them."

APPENDIX B

Guidelines for Sharing

- Speak only for yourself about beliefs, feelings, and responses.

- Respect and receive what others offer, even if you disagree.

- Listening is more important than talking. Avoid cross-talk, interrupting, speaking for others, or trying to "fix" another person's problems.

- Honor the different ways God works in individuals.

- Do not be afraid of silence. Use it to listen to the Spirit in your midst.

- Maintain confidentiality. What is shared in the group stays in the group.

- Recognize that all group members have permission to share only what and when they are ready to share.

From *Companions in Christ: A Small-Group Experience in Spiritual Formation*, Leader's Guide (Nashville, TN: Upper Room Books, 2001), 14.

MORE TIPS

- The rituals for beginning and ending the session provide a way for people to transition from everyday life to this gathering and back to everyday life. Rituals also help the group start and end on time.

- Include some "gathering time" to ease the transition into each session. If someone has had a particularly full week, you may need to modify the session's time line. If more time is needed, suggest that the conversation continue after the closing.

- Be sure to read and talk through each of the points above at your first session and refer to them again at least once (we suggest doing this during the third session). Many problems that groups experience will diminish if they follow these guidelines. Reading them together takes the pressure off the leader to be the "enforcer of the rules" and makes them normative for good group interaction.

- Some people will feel more comfortable sharing with one person rather than the total group; for that reason, we include one-on-one time for each session. Depending on the size and comfort level of the group, you may want to increase or decrease that portion of the meeting.

- Participants may need to ask the question, "How will we honor what happens in our group between sessions?" This becomes a particularly important issue for discussion if group members interact with one another in other arenas, such as members of a church staff.

APPENDIX C

Congregational Assessment of the Fruit of the Spirit
(Based on Galatians 5:22-23)

Where in the last six months have you seen evidence of the fruit of the Spirit?
I have seen the fruit of **love** in my congregation in the following places:

I have seen the fruit of **joy** in my congregation in the following places:

I have seen **peace** in my congregation in these ways:

I have seen **patience** in my congregation (we have "waited upon the LORD" in these ways):

I have seen **kindness** in my congregation (where and how):

Here are some examples of where I have seen **goodness** at my church:

I have seen **faithfulness** in my congregation in the following ways:

I have seen **gentleness** in my congregation in these ways:

I have seen self-control exercised in the following circumstances:

Thanks to Robert C. Morris for permission to publish this survey; he is available for questions or comments at angelhold@earthlink.net

APPENDIX D

Suggestions for Clergy Groups

Both of us (Trevor and Jerry) are ordained clergy, and both of us have presented the Cycle of Grace to clergy groups. Clergy are sometimes a difficult group to reach, but we have found a strong, positive response to the Cycle of Grace in our various settings. While the concept is easily grasped, it offers enough nuance to intrigue most people.

Trevor presented the complete outline of the Cycle of Grace in an hour to a group of clergy gathered for The Upper Room's Companions in Ministry retreat. It was a rich hour of insight, conversation, laughter, and more than a few "aha" moments. Then the pastors were sent off for an hour of silence to reflect on what they had heard. Upon their return, they shared more willingly about moments of pain as well as joy in their personal lives and in their ministries.

Jerry presented the Cycle of Grace at a twenty-four-hour clergy retreat. Since this was his first time with the group, he used the first hour to share some of his struggles that led to burnout in the ministry before launching into the presentation on the Cycle of Grace and the initial movement of grace, Acceptance. As the participants entered thirty minutes of silence, Jerry invited them to reflect on the question, "What grounds you in God's love and acceptance in your life and ministry? To what do you return to claim your identity as a beloved child of God?" The pastors then were invited to share their responses, and a service reaffirming the baptismal covenant followed. That evening the participants worked in small groups to create a list of "sustaining practices" in Jesus' life, tagging those that sounded like practices they might want to try. The next morning the group worked through the rest of the Cycle, beginning with Significance, followed by Fruitfulness, and ending with the Cycle of Works.

In our work with clergy groups, we are keenly aware of the potential for "shop talk" and gripe sessions. Clergy often want and need positive spiritual environments in which to share their lives, yet the lack of trust holds them back. In his book *A Hidden Wholeness*, Parker Palmer compares the soul to a wild animal.[1] A wild animal is very shy, coming to the waterhole only when it's safe and still. In a similar way, the souls of clergy need stillness and safety to move from "role talk" to "soul talk."[2]

For Companions in Ministry, Jerry and the design team intentionally recruited an ecumenical mix of clergy to lower the risk of extended conversations about denominational politics. We also organized the group so that half were clergywomen and half were clergymen. While challenging to some, most recognized the need for a different perspective on life and ministry. Break-out sessions and meals provided time for women and men to gather in same gender groups if they wished. Participation by various racial ethnic leaders and persons with disabilities added much to these conversations.

Helpful and constructive clergy groups don't just happen. Too often well-meaning denominational leaders want clergy to get together in small groups and then organize or require such gatherings. We think a better place to start is within oneself. When clergy identify specific persons with whom to form a small group, the group will have a better chance of faring well because of its friendship or companionship basis. For many clergy this approach is a new idea. We clergy often feel obliged to colleagues struggling in ministry or in their personal lives. Or we don't believe building good collegial relationships is important enough for us to prioritize in our lives, so we wait until we're forced to do it. Then we're stuck in a group where we may not fit. Better to take initiative and organize the group you want.

Our prayers go with you as you begin this journey. We know the difficulties of ministry, but we also know the abundance of God's grace, working within you in more ways that you can ever ask or imagine.

1. Parker J. Palmer, *A Hidden Wholeness: The Journey toward an Undivided Life* (San Francisco: Jossey-Bass, 2004), 58 and following.
2. Ibid., chapter 2. While the soul needs a place to talk, Palmer correctly points to the need for "soul" and "role" to be rejoined.

ABOUT THE AUTHORS

TREVOR HUDSON has ministered at Northfield Methodist Church in Benoni, South Africa, for the past twenty years and travels widely to conduct conferences, workshops, and retreats. He is the well-known author of ten titles, including *Journey of the Spirit*, which received the Christian Booksellers' Association of South Africa's award for Best Christian Publication in 2000. *The Serenity Prayer* is one of several of his works that has been published internationally in different languages. Upper Room Books has also published *One Day at a Time* (a companion to the Serenity Prayer) and more recently, *Questions God Asks*. You can follow Trevor on Twitter @ trevor040451.

JERRY P. HAAS pastored churches in California and Arizona for twenty-five years and then moved to Nashville, Tennessee, to work in retreat and spiritual formation ministries with The Upper Room/General Board of Discipleship. He served as project coordinator for *Upper Room Worshipbook: Music and Liturgies for Spiritual Formation*, coeditor of *Rhythm & Fire: Experiencing the Holy in Community and Solitude*; and coauthor of *Shaping a Life of Significance for Retirement* with R. Jack Hansen. He and his wife, Donna, now reside in the Tucson, Arizona area. He can be reached at jndhaas@gmail.com

CPSIA information can be obtained
at www.ICGtesting.com
Printed in the USA
LVHW021120051218
599328LV00001B/1/P